RETURN TO THE ....ATION

Return
To The Island
Of Occupation

Robert Plant

JOHN RITCHIE LTD
CHRISTIAN PUBLICATIONS

40 Beansburn, Kilmarnock, Scotland

ISBN-13: 978 1 910513 48 4

Copyright © 2016 by John Ritchie Ltd.
40 Beansburn, Kilmarnock, Scotland

www.ritchiechristianmedia.co.uk

Typeset by John Ritchie Ltd., Kilmarnock
Printed by Bell & Bain Ltd., Glasgow

Dedication

For my big sister
Anita
Who spent her formative years in
Pont du Val, St Brelade, Jersey
and like the author has returned to the island often.

Contents

Return To The Island Of Occupation

Map of Jersey

CHAPTER 1

The warm September sun shone upon the golden sands that stretched along the shore at Sandown. Jerry and Linda felt the rays on their backs as they looked longingly at the forbidden beach. It had been heavily mined in order to help prevent any attempted German invasion and was out of bounds to anyone other than soldiers. The two forlorn young teenagers sighed as they lifted their eyes and gazed out to sea – out towards their homes, on the distant and enemy-occupied Island of Jersey.

The summer of 1941 was drawing to a close. It had been two months since Jerry and Linda had risked everything to escape from Jersey in a small boat with the important information that Adolf Hitler, the German leader, was planning to make a visit to Jersey. The two friends, along with others, had thought that when the German leader made the fifteen-mile crossing from the coast of France to the previously insignificant Channel Island of Jersey, he would be very vulnerable, hence making him an easy target for the Allied forces. How disappointed and disillusioned they had been when arriving in London they discovered that not only were Hitler's plans already known by British intelligence, they had been cancelled. Hitler would not be venturing out of the safety of Germany after all.

Despair had initially gripped them. To think that their great endeavour had all been for nothing! To add to the great feeling of misery was their fear for Jerry's Uncle Fred. He had been captured by the Germans on the Island of Guernsey whilst attempting to get more fuel for their boat. As the two scanned the horizon, they still had no idea whether Uncle Fred was dead or alive.

They had now been waiting on the Isle of Wight for over a month and the school holidays were at an end. Long days of studying in a strange school, on a strange island and with strange people loomed ahead of them.

With their thoughts still far across the sea, Linda and Jerry began the long walk from the little town of Sandown on the east coast, past the large town of Shanklin, and on towards their temporary home just outside the village of Godshill.

"My word, you two do look down in the dumps," came a voice from a small, slightly stooped, elderly lady who carried across her arm a basket filled to the brim with apples.

It was Linda who spoke first. "We were just thinking about starting school on Monday and wondering how our families are."

"Your families?" the old lady questioned. "Are you not living here with your families?"

"No, we're not," Jerry butted in with resentment. "Our families live in Jersey and we are staying with Mr and Mrs Griffiths up in Godshill."

"Oh!" the lady replied as a light suddenly came upon her wizened face. "So you must be the two children who came here from Jersey?"

"Yes, we are and we really want to go back home and find out whether our families are safe. We don't want to have to start school again on Monday," came Linda's despondent reply.

"Don't you like school, then?"

"Oh, we don't mind it, but we just wonder how our families are getting on and whether we will ever see home again," Jerry replied, softening his tone.

"Well, I'm over eighty and I saw the last war and I wouldn't think there is much hope of you getting back there while this war is on. To be honest, I think you're better off here in safety without your family than in a country occupied by those Nazis." The old lady straightened herself and looked at the two youngsters through her glasses rather quizzically.

"Yes, you're probably right – there's not much hope of

getting home except by parachute and I don't expect the RAF would be too willing to take us in a plane and parachute us out over Jersey!" Jerry responded half-jokingly, but half hoping that maybe somebody, somewhere, would think of some way of getting them home.

"I don't think the Germans would be too happy either." Linda tried to laugh. "They'd probably think the invasion had started and shoot us dead before we landed."

"Yes, you're right, Linda. There's no chance of us getting home," Jerry replied dejectedly. "Well, at least we know we'd be in heaven if we did get shot," he added, trying to be more cheerful.

"My advice is just stay here on the Isle of Wight till the war is over and then you'll be able to get back to see your families in safety. It's a beautiful island, do you not think?"

"Well, it's not bad," Linda replied. "It's just too big to walk round if you want to get anywhere. In Jersey we could easily walk across the Island and back in a day but everything here is so far away!"

The old woman gave a chuckle. "Just be glad they've not placed you in England or Scotland, then you would have something to complain about. Anyway, I'd better be on my way. You two take care and don't risk anything you don't have to. Your lives are very important."

"Don't worry about us. We'll be just fine," Linda replied as she and Jerry continued up the road that led to their temporary home. "Goodbye," she called behind her.

After walking about half a mile in silence, Linda turned to Jerry. "Do you think we'll be staying here until the end of the war like that lady said?"

"Stay here without knowing if Mum and Dad are okay. Absolutely not, I intend to go back. Just think though if it had been true about Hitler's trip to Jersey the war would have been over by now," Jerry retorted angrily kicking at a small stone. "You can stay here in safety if you want, but I'm going home to Jersey, come what may. The only problem is that I haven't as yet found the right way to get there."

"You're not going on your own," Linda replied indignantly. "If you go, I'll go with you."

A silence descended on them again as they carried on walking along the hedge-lined road that wound through lush green fields. Linda, a usually cheerful, chatty girl, soon gave in to her thoughts. "You know, when we left Jersey all we could think about was getting safely here with our news and getting Hitler assassinated. Now all we want to do is get home and know that everything is okay, but things are just not looking quite so straightforward."

Following a perilous journey across the English Channel, the children had been discovered, washed up on the Isle of Wight, by British soldiers. With the vital information they carried, they had been quickly whisked to London in order to pass it on to the Allied authorities in the Big City, accompanied by two soldiers: Sergeant Cuthbert Rennoldson and a medical corporal called Brian Oliver. After much persuasion from the children, the two soldiers had managed to break, bend or twist every rule in order to find the two refugees accommodation on the Isle of Wight. Concerned for their families, Jerry and Linda both wanted desperately to return to their home in Jersey. The Isle of Wight, situated off the south coast of England, seemed the best place for the return part of their adventure to begin.

Cuthbert and Brian were also both stationed on the island and despite their reservations had wondered if they would be able to assist the two children to return to Jersey. With increased fighting, almost weekly air raids and dangers from German ships working out of captured harbours in France, the chances of getting back to Jersey did not look good.

As the children arrived at the open whitewashed front door of the quaint old-fashioned guesthouse where they were staying, a hand carrying a large yellow cloth shot out, waving it almost in the faces of the two youngsters. "Hey up! Steady on," laughed Jerry as he and Linda sought to duck out of the way. "We don't want dusting as well, you know."

The duster abruptly stopped flapping about and a lady turned towards them, speaking with a soft Welsh accent. "Oh, I'm so sorry, dears! I was chatting to Geoff and not concentrating on what I was doing."

The two children smiled at the lady they had become very fond of over the five weeks they had been staying in Beacon Cottage. Mrs Griffiths was a jolly lady who always seemed to be busy doing something – cleaning, polishing, mending or out working in her neat and tidy garden. Although not big in height, she had a well-rounded figure which both children agreed made her look rather like a rugby ball on legs as she waddled along the streets at great speed.

Mr and Mrs Griffiths had moved to the Isle of Wight over thirty years before to start up a small bed and breakfast business. They had lived in the town of Treherbert in the Rhondda Valley in Wales. Geoff had wanted to get out of working down the mines and the Isle of Wight had seemed the perfect place to open a guesthouse.

"Come in, come in," she enthused as she ushered Jerry and Linda through the front door. "Would you like a nice drink of freshly-pressed apple juice and one of my Welsh cakes? They nodded enthusiastically at the offer. Mrs Griffith's Welsh cakes were well known in the locality and the children devoured as many as they could when they were offered. As they waited in the cosy living room with its beamed ceiling, they suddenly started to feel a little better about life, especially when Mrs Griffiths appeared with the tray containing two glasses of ice-cold cloudy apple juice and a plate overloaded with Welsh cakes.

"There you are, now," their hostess spoke heartily. "You enjoy these while the cakes are still warm and the apple is still cold."

"Oh, thank you, Mrs Griffiths. You're the best," Linda replied, reaching out to take one of the two glasses on the tray.

"Um, so you keep saying, but I'm a very poor replacement for your parents, you know. That said, I've never had children of my own and you two make good company for my Geoff and I. With this war on, there's not too many folks keen to take a holiday anywhere and most of our young men are in the services fighting for king and country. So it's nice having you two round the place...you sort of brighten it up with your fun and cheerful smiles!"

"Well, don't be too surprised if we are grumpy and scowling on Monday when school starts," Jerry replied as he reached out for a Welsh cake. "I'm not sure I'll be feeling very happy at having to start school again, doing mathematics and writing with children I don't know. In fact, I'm not looking forward to it at all."

"Oh, you'll be all right. The children here on the island are not so bad, you know. You could have been sent somewhere else where the children might not have been as friendly. I'm sure it will all work out for you."

"I suppose we will find out for ourselves on Monday what the children on the Isle of Wight are really like," Jerry said with a sigh.

"We'll just have to get on with it and make the best of it. It looks like we'll be here for a while," Linda replied, trying to be realistic.

"There'll no doubt be some sort of adventure lurking round the corner with you around, Linda," Jerry smiled.

"I just worry that one day I'll get up and you will both have disappeared, trying to get back home," interjected Mrs Griffiths.

"Don't you worry, Mrs Griffiths. We'll let you know if we start out on that sort of adventure. Anyway, Cuthbert and Brian won't let us do anything even marginally dangerous so you can be sure that we will be quite safe," Linda replied, smiling reassuringly at the older lady.

"And," Jerry added with all seriousness, "we will have God to help us in everything we do, and if we have Him we really need nothing more."

"Um, well, I'm not underestimating the power of God at all, I saw it myself forty years ago during one of the great Welsh revivals, but God will not just step in and help you if you decide to do something daft like sailing back to Jersey on your own."

Just then the doorbell rang, reverberating with a loud *ding-dong* from the two bells that hung over the top of the front door. "Oh my, now someone is here and I'm still wearing my baking apron," Mrs Griffiths groaned in horror as she scurried out of the room and into the hallway.

As soon as the door was opened, both children heard familiar voices resonating off the oak-panelled walls of the hall. They immediately jumped up as their two good army friends, Cuthbert and Brian, made a noisy entrance.

"I've some great news!" Cuthbert said excitedly as he came towards them. "My captain has received word that your uncle is alive and is in Guernsey. He's recovering from being shot in his shoulder, but other than that, as far as we know, he is fine. I'm not sure how the communiqué was received but we're sure it's absolutely true."

"Oh, thank goodness," breathed Linda, letting out a sigh that she felt had been pent up inside her since Uncle Fred's capture by the Germans. "We had no idea whether he was dead or alive."

"That really is just the best news ever," Jerry said ecstatically.

CHAPTER 2

"Well," Jerry said as the two friends finished supper that night, "just one more day before school starts."

"Oh, don't remind me. Please, please don't mention school to me again," Linda wailed with a frown on her usually cheerful countenance. "At least not until Monday morning."

Monday arrived far too quickly and the children found themselves walking the short distance to the village school. They slowed as they neared the old stone building with its sandy-coloured walls and grey roof. Mrs Griffiths had already informed them that the school had been in existence since the 1600s and was one of the oldest on the island. As they scanned its arched doorway and large windows, they wondered if anything inside had changed since its first pupils had arrived, over three hundred years ago.

"Hello, there!" a faint voice called out to them from inside the building. Both children looked across in the direction of the school, but apart from seeing a couple of other pupils entering through the school gate they could see no one.

"Hello," the voice called again, as they heard a loud clatter and saw a large sash window fly open at the front of the building. This produced a cloud of dust which enveloped a middle-aged woman inside, who was obviously standing on a chair.

"Hello, Jerry and Linda!" the friendly voice called a third time. As a face appeared through the rapidly-disappearing dust, both children recognised the lady as the headmistress, Mrs Turner. They had been introduced to Mrs Turner the previous week when she came to visit them at Mrs Griffiths'. "It's good to see you both again," she continued. "Just wait in the entrance. I'll be there in a jiffy."

As she swept into view in her long, grey, pleated dress, she was gushing with enthusiasm. "I saw you from the classroom and just had to say hello, then that stupid window stuck as I tried to open it and covered me in dust. Never mind. It probably won't close now!" She brushed furiously at her dress and then continued, "There's always something goes wrong on the first day back after the holidays."

Her infectious chatter made Jerry and Linda smile and they were beginning to wonder if maybe this new school wouldn't be too bad after all. She led her new charges into their classroom. As they entered, a young female teacher, dressed in a white blouse and red full-length skirt, looked up from a book she was reading.

"These," gushed Mrs Turner, "are our two heroes from the Channel Islands."

"Oh, pleased to meet you," the young teacher responded, smiling enthusiastically at the children. "I have been so looking forward to seeing you two, and cannot wait to hear all about your adventure..."

"Hopefully they will tell us all about that later," Mrs Turner interrupted. She glanced encouragingly at the two children, but before giving them a chance to reply she continued, "Well, for now I'll let you all get on. I must see to my own class," and breezed quickly out of the large, airy classroom, her skirt swishing as she went.

"Let's find your desks." The young teacher motioned to Linda as she walked down the classroom. "Here's yours, Linda, and this one is yours, Jerry." She pointed to two wooden desks, one behind the other, with lift-up tops. "Now, you are very welcome in this school and I hope that you will be very happy in my class. I'm Miss Matherson, by the way."

"Thank you," replied Linda, who suddenly realised for the first time that about ten other children were watching her and Jerry rather suspiciously.

"I was wondering if later on this morning you would tell the whole class how you came to arrive on the Isle of Wight. I'm sure they will all be very interested. It will also help them to get to know you a little."

"Um…" Jerry stuttered. "I…I don't know…maybe another time." Jerry knew that neither he nor Linda would want to stand in front of the whole class and repeat the details of their journey from Jersey to England.

"Nonsense, nonsense." Mrs Turner reappeared at the door with a large brown envelope for Miss Matherson. "The whole school would like to be invited in to listen."

Linda, knowing exactly what Jerry was thinking, said, "I think, Mrs Turner, that we'd be happier just keeping the story to ourselves."

Mrs Turner protested again, "No, no, no! There is absolutely no need to be shy. It's not often a hero arrives in my school and to have two actually studying here is too good to be true. I'll tell the other teacher to come here with her children just before lunch; I'm sure you can tell something of your great adventures to us all."

Linda caught sight of Jerry screwing his face up in total disapproval of the idea, and Linda's own stomach started to knot as she thought of having to tell their story to all the children in the school. She said nothing but quietly took her seat behind the allocated desk.

Mrs Turner having disappeared, Linda turned round to see Jerry who still had a look of bewilderment on his face. "What are we going to do?" he whispered.

"I don't know. Mrs Turner didn't seem to want to listen to…Speak to you at play time…" Her voice died away as Miss Matherson rapped on her desk to get the attention of all the children.

The morning was very similar to schooldays they had known back home in Jersey. There were the usual maths questions, some English work, along with the usual list of spellings, and a bit of geography when Miss Matherson showed the class where Jerry and Linda had come from.

At break time the two got together to discuss the problem they had of telling their adventure to the school. "Do you think we should go and see Mrs Turner to tell her we don't want to tell everyone our story? I mean, it could put our families in danger if everybody knows," Linda suggested apprehensively.

"I don't think she'll listen," Jerry answered, smiling weakly. "She wouldn't this morning when I tried to argue with her."

"She does speak rather fast. Maybe she didn't hear you."

"Oh, she heard all right. She just didn't want to hear," Jerry asserted. "I've never stood up and spoken to lots of people like that before, but you have. Remember that time you had to speak about your dad's old tractor. Maybe you should do it."

"But that was in front of my friends, those I'd known right through school, but we don't know anyone here. Anyway, Jerry, this is definitely a case of boys before girls!"

"Hum! Thanks very much!" Jerry replied dejectedly.

"Hey, just a minute. I've got an idea," Linda announced as a smile started to play around her lips. "Why don't we tell them about how we found God instead?"

"Yes, that's an idea," Jerry concurred. "That was a real adventure. We could tell about how we started out looking for England and ended up finding God. Mind you, they will probably all laugh at us."

"So what," Linda said. "I'm sure that somehow God will help you to say what you need to say, Jerry."

Jerry was still not keen on the idea. However, he felt they really had very little option.

"Okay," he acknowledged. "I'll do it, but you'll have to help me a bit. If you can sort of get me started, I'll try and carry on from there."

Both children felt happier when they had settled on Linda's plan about what they were going to say once midday arrived.

At the agreed time, another twenty-one children of all ages squashed into the classroom. Linda and Jerry were made to stand at the front with Mrs Turner, whilst Miss Matherson and another teacher stood at the back to help keep all the children under control.

"Now then, children," Mrs Turner said as she clapped her hands to gain their attention. "You must all have heard about the two heroes from Jersey who risked their lives to bring important news about the war from their Island to England. You know they were shot at by German soldiers and had to steer an open boat right up the Channel and then swam to shore in a terrible storm at Freshwater Bay. I think they walked over a beach that was mined without getting killed. Is that not right, Jerry and Linda?" She looked at them but didn't wait for a reply. "So you can see why I call them our two heroes! I'm so very glad that they will be attending our school until the war is won. Now they are going to fill us in on all the details of their amazing adventure." She smiled at the two children who were now extremely nervous. Their plans of what they'd hoped to say seemed as if they weren't going to work out.

Linda, not quite knowing what else to do, stuttered in a soft hoarse voice, "We...are not sure really what to say." As she viewed the other children sitting in front of her, her legs became more like jelly and her mouth was dry. "It's...it's... just that we had some news that we knew was important about the war and we brought it up from Jersey and landed at Freshwater Bay."

There was a pause before Jerry realised he needed to say something. "That's really all there is to it," Jerry added rather desperately, hoping they'd provided enough information to keep Mrs Turner happy.

"No, no," Mrs Turner chipped in. "We want to know all about your adventure across the sea and everything that happened to you."

"Oh...Okay." Linda began to feel a bit more confident and started again. "Well...you see...Jerry's Uncle Fred helped us. He used to be a real wild sailor." She decided maybe it was easier to tell someone else's story. "He was always drunk, fighting and in trouble, but one day in Belfast he heard someone preaching about the love of God and forgiveness of sins and he became a Christian."

Jerry, emboldened by Linda's apparent confidence of telling about Uncle Fred, took over. "Yes, and becoming a Christian made him a changed person, always reading his Bible, praying and trying to help others. It all happened one night during the last war. He missed his ship and had to stay in Belfast. When he finally got back to Southampton he found that his ship had been sunk by a German U-boat. There were no survivors. So he used to say he was saved twice in one night – once from sin and once from the sea."

Jerry paused and glanced properly for the first time at his audience. They seemed to be paying attention. He then looked at Linda for further encouragement. Seeing her looking back, he went on, more boldly than ever, "Well, Uncle Fred, he offered to help us escape from Jersey and come over here. Before we left Jersey in our little boat he read his Bible to us, and also prayed to God to protect us.

Then on our way here we had to get more fuel in Guernsey. He had managed to climb the cliffs and throw some of the fuel cans down to us, but he was caught by the Germans. We didn't know what to do, but heard him calling to us to carry on without him.

After we had sailed away from Guernsey we found his Bible in the bottom of the boat and it had a bookmark in a page in John's gospel. On the page, two parts were underlined and they said, 'Let not your heart be troubled: ye believe in God, believe also in Me,' and then a bit further down, it said, 'Jesus saith unto him, "I am the way, the truth, and the life: no man cometh unto the Father, but by Me." ' "

Jerry hesitated. He seemed to get stuck at this point. A lump was forming in his throat as he recalled his uncle being caught by the Germans.

Linda knew she had to take over. "Well, as Jerry steered the boat up the Channel," she continued with increasing confidence, "we decided that this must be sort of a code from the Lord Jesus to us. We thought He was saying not to worry as everything would work out okay in the end. Then He was telling us that He was the way to heaven. We then worked out that He was the only way to heaven because He died on the cross to save us from sin. Sins are the bad things we do."

Jerry, having composed himself, spoke again. "Linda was much quicker than me at realising the importance of what the Lord Jesus was saying in the Bible, and when we were staying in a bed and breakfast in London she trusted Him as her Saviour. The next morning after breakfast, I realised that God had sent us from Jersey, not so much to tell others about Hitler's coming to visit the Island of Jersey, but so that He could make us understand our need to be right with God and ready for heaven. So once I had realised this, I trusted Him too. Now we know that we are both forgiven by God and going to heaven." He looked around; his audience seemed to expect him to go on. "That's really all there is to our story."

There was a silence in the classroom as Mrs Turner, for the first time that morning, seemed to be at a loss for words. "Ah, um, most, er, shall we say, interesting and er, um, not at all what I was really expecting or – how can I put it? – what I thought you'd say."

"Well, we did get a bit lost in the English Channel, and we could have been killed when the Germans shot at us as we were leaving Jersey," Linda calmly added.

Jerry looked up again at the children. "We could also tell you a bit about the storm that washed us up in Freshwater Bay too, but we've told you the really important things."

When they both sat down, they were amazed that they had been able to say so much so boldly.

"However did we manage that?" Jerry whispered, his hands shaking with fear and his legs feeling like lead weights.

"I think God gave us help," Linda answered simply as she rubbed her still-knotted stomach.

CHAPTER 3

At lunchtime, the two newcomers tried to find out a bit more about the school. As they asked questions, they discovered that there were thirty-seven pupils in the school, all between the ages of six and fifteen, and that they were two of the older pupils. Linda looked around at the old stone walls and high ceilings, remembering what Mrs Griffiths had told her about its history, and wondering just how many children had been taught there over the years.

"Actually, the school originated in 1615," Miss Matherson explained as she showed Jerry and Linda around the small building. "There used to be an estate near here which was owned by the Worsley family, and it was Lady Ann Worsley who wanted to commence the school. Since then, her family, along with the Earl of Yarborough, has had close ties with the school. Another descendent of the Worsley family, built this building in the early 1800s, so this school building is about one hundred and thirty years old."

"Wow," said Jerry, spinning on his heels and looking all around him. "Wouldn't it be just amazing if you could speak to some of the first pupils who ever attended this school? Then we could find out what things were like when they were here."

"Ah, well," Miss Matherson replied, "my old grandmother has a saying that 'time and death wait for no man' and the more I think about it, the more true it seems to be, especially with our boys out there fighting Hitler's army. Now, off with you into the playground and make some friends."

Jerry and Linda pushed open the big oak door that led out into the cobbled yard at the side of the school, where children were playing hopscotch and whip and top. Some girls even had homemade hoops which they were trying to keep spinning around their waists for as long as possible.

"Oy, you!" called a stocky boy with wavy black hair. He looked slightly older than Jerry. "Come 'ere," he called again, as he leaned casually up against a stone wall.

Jerry sauntered cautiously over to the lad, replying with a cheery, "Hello."

"You think you're really *it*, don't you?" sneered the boy as he straightened up and towered over Jerry in an attempt to intimidate him. "Me and my mates think you and your girlfriend there are just a couple of attention seekers. We don't believe that story about escaping from Jersey or any of that rubbish about God. Just remember, this is our school and our island and you're not welcome. Understand?"

"I thought everyone here was supposed to be friendly and kind," Linda spoke rather boldly as she came towards the boy to try to help Jerry out.

"Listen," the big lad growled, "I make all the noise round here so you two just keep quiet and don't try to take over."

"Who said anything about taking over?" Jerry questioned.

"I did! I saw how Mrs Turner was sweet on you two when you arrived."

"Well, that's not our fault."

"Yes, it is. You arrived here where we don't want you. So just keep out of my way or there will be big trouble." He stopped and then added, "That's both of you!"

"Who is that big lad in the other class?" Linda enquired of Miss Matherson before they left for home at the end of the day.

"Oh, you mean MM! Michael Meddlum," Miss Matherson answered with a knowing look. "Just be careful of him as he is big in every way – size, mouth and ego!"

"So we found out at lunchtime," Linda answered.

"I shouldn't be saying it, but he has another name in the village – Michael Meddling. He always has his nose in other people's business so just be very careful."

"Okay, we will keep well clear of him. Thanks for the advice, Miss Matherson."

"That's no problem. We don't really want you two explorers to have any more big adventures, especially any involving Michael Meddlum! Now be on your way and we'll see you in the morning."

Jerry and Linda said goodbye and made their way out of the school and up the road to their Isle of Wight home.

"Phewee," exclaimed Mrs Griffiths, pursing her lips tightly together before continuing. "Michael Meddlum, what a lad! Very sad, really. His dad's away in the navy, has been for years. His mother's got no control over Michael at all, just lets him do what he likes." She paused as she lifted the china teapot. "Any more tea for anyone?" She poured out another cup for herself. "I have apple pie in the oven too."

"Yummy! I thought I could smell something good," Jerry answered. "Is there custard too?"

"Hang on, young man," Mr Griffiths responded with a chuckle from the other side of the table. "There is a war on, you know, so don't be expecting too much. It's hard enough for Blodwyn to get the flour to make some pastry never mind to add custard as well."

"I'm sorry," Jerry answered, feeling rather ashamed. "It's just that I love custard with apple pie."

"That's all right, my dear," Mrs Griffiths smiled. "I'll go and get the pie."

Within a few minutes, the four of them tucked into the delicious pie.

"Yes, you two just keep out of that boy's way as much as you can," Mrs Griffiths said, returning to the subject of Michael Meddlum. "I'd love to say if you keep out of his way, he'll keep out of yours, but Michael isn't like that. He's always sticking his nose in where it's not wanted and getting himself and others into trouble."

"That's what Miss Matherson said. She said that MM stands for Michael Meddling."

"Well, to think a teacher said that about a pupil!" Mrs Griffiths replied as a smile played on her round face and a glint of mischief came into her eye. "She's right, of course, and is just trying to keep you two safe. What that boy needs is a good dose of old-fashioned discipline with a belt across his backside like I used to have. That's what he needs, he does," she repeated to make sure that she'd got the message across.

By the end of the week, school had become a normal way of life for the two refugees, and although they missed home and family, the majority of the children in the school had been kind to them and asked lots of questions about their adventures.

Saturday dawned bright and clear and Mrs Griffiths suggested that Jerry and Linda walk up to the coastal town of Ventnor for the day. She proposed they make themselves a packed lunch and take plenty of time to explore the town. "It's a bit different than it was before the war. There is a radar station there which the Luftwaffe keep trying to destroy so it's had a few air raids and a few bombs dropped on it, but you should hopefully enjoy yourselves."

After a bustling half hour making up some cheese and pickle sandwiches, boiling eggs and buttering a bit of dry fruit bread, they set off across the green fields that led over the hill at Stenbury Down to drop down the other side towards their destination. As they came to the top, they looked out over the land towards the sea.

"Will we ever get back home?" Linda asked wistfully.

"I don't really know, but I am sure if there's a way Brian and Cuthbert will be trying their hardest to find it." Jerry picked up a small piece of chalk and threw it across the field. "I like the Isle of Wight but I do worry about what could happen to Mum and Dad when the Germans find we're gone...and they will find out sometime."

"I know. My mum and dad already had a close shave with the Gestapo. The sooner we can get back, the sooner they will be safe. I just wonder what the Germans might do to us, though, when we do get there," Linda replied. "I suppose if God kept us safe coming here, He can do the same for us returning too," she concluded, then she looked at Jerry. "Come on, race you to Ventnor." They both began to run as fast as they could down the far side of the hill towards the track that led to Ventnor.

"Oy, you two! Come 'ere," a rough voice called to them as they neared a wooded area alongside the track.

The two of them stopped dead as Michael Meddlum appeared out of the woods along with three other teenagers, one a girl that Jerry and Linda did not recognise.

"What you doing on my hill?" Michael enquired in his harsh manner.

"What do you mean *your hill*?" Jerry asked.

"This land is all mine and you're not allowed on it, so why are you here?" the big lad scowled as he strode purposefully towards them.

"We were told by Mrs Griffiths that this down belonged to the Worsley family," Linda responded.

"Well, it don't, do it? It belongs to my dad. He's not happy about strangers like you two running all over his land, so he wants me and my friends here to teach you both a lesson." Then turning to the others, he said, "Right, let's get them."

Before Jerry knew what was happening, someone had leapt on his back and thrown their arms around his neck, clamping them tightly round him. Linda acted instinctively and tried to pull the lad off Jerry's back. As she did so, the girl grabbed her hair and pulled her to the ground. The two friends struggled with their four assailants in an unequal fight against older and stronger children.

Linda ended up face down on the ground as the older girl rubbed her face hard in the grass and pulled her hair. She tried to kick back with her legs but was unable to reach the girl who pinned her to the ground.

Jerry really had little chance as he tried to protect himself from the three boys who held, pummelled and punched him.

Eventually, Linda managed to wriggle free of her captor and rugby-tackled Michael to the ground, winding him badly as he landed on the chalk track. In no time, another of the boys was on her back, pinning her hands behind her. Linda just had time to think about praying for help and calling out, "Lord, save us," when the boy holding her down suddenly let go.

"Stop, this instant! What on earth is going on?" a familiar voice bellowed with authority.

Turning herself round and sitting up, Linda exclaimed, "Brian!" The army medic they had befriended now held the struggling and protesting boy that a few seconds earlier had been pinning her to the ground.

"What sort of a man are you?" Brian growled at the young man he held in his grasp. The young man remained silent with his head bowed.

"They started it," complained Michael, as he got up from the ground.

"Aye, and you'd really expect me to believe that of these two, wouldn't you, Michael Meddlum?"

"Hey, how do you know my name?" the youngster whined.

"Never mind how. What I want to know is what's going on?"

Michael looked at the ground and kicked the stones on the path. Jerry held his jaw where he had been punched and tried to get his breath.

Brian concentrated his gaze on Michael and spoke again, "Someone had better start telling the truth, because from what I witnessed just now and the way I feel, there might just be more blood shed here than only Jerry's split lip." Brian looked at Jerry wiping blood away from his mouth, then asked, "Jerry, Linda, do you want to tell us what was going on? Michael seems to have lost his tongue. As I drove up the track it seemed that it was a pretty unfair fight of four against two. You were all so involved that you never even heard my jeep approaching."

"I think you should ask them, really," replied Jerry.

"Well?" Brian questioned, looking at the boy he still held tightly.

"It were Michael's idea," the boy eventually answered in a low, hoarse whisper.

"Well, Michael, you'd better start explaining, and explaining quickly."

"Well…er, ah…you see," the boy stammered as he continued kicking a stone, "it was just a bit of fun that got out of hand."

Brian shook his head in disgust. "Michael, you're a rotten liar! Everyone round here knows you're a bully and trouble, so no more lies. I want the truth!"

"Please, sir," the boy still being held by Brian spoke out. "Michael didn't like these two and he reckoned what everyone was saying about them travelling up from Jersey was just lies. I think Michael was just jealous because everyone was talking about them and saying how brave they had been." He paused as he looked across at Michael. "He told us we had to teach them a lesson when we saw them coming across the down, sort of duff them up a little."

Michael glared at his friend with a fierce scowl.

Brian in turn gave Michael such a look that he quickly looked down at the ground again.

"Thanks for that, son. Now we are getting somewhere. What's your name?"

"David Penhurst," the lad said, with a pained expression on his face.

"Well, I need to see your parents. I think they will be horrified to learn that you were not only picking on, but also holding a girl younger than yourself face down to the ground. I hope they give you what you deserve. Now, scoot, before I set on you myself." He let go of the boy who needed no second bidding to run up the hill away from the others. "You two clear off with him," he continued as he motioned to the others, "and I advise you to find better friends next time."

Then, turning to Michael as he attempted to join the others

in retreat, he said, "Not you, you big bully! You stay here. I want a word with you, you coward."

Jerry and Linda watched Brian march Michael towards his jeep and then hold him against the vehicle's side. The soldier's voice was stern and deep as he growled at the now very frightened and subdued boy. "Michael Meddlum, if I so much as get another sniff of you causing any more trouble, I'll march you straight to the nearest police station. I'll be writing a full report about your little escapade today and presenting it to my commanding officer. I'll ask him to keep it, but if you cause just one more ounce of trouble, that will be passed to the police too. I hate bullies and you're about the worst I have seen. I'd love to give you a real dose of your own medicine but maybe, just maybe, when I speak to your mother and your friends' parents that will be enough of a punishment for you. Now, go! Get out of my sight. Run up the hill and don't dare stop until you're over the other side!"

"I thought you were going to march him away to shoot him," Linda stated.

"Oh, no! I wouldn't have done that," Brian replied as he watched the stocky frame of Michael running for all he was worth across the down. "Mind you, I felt like it!"

"I'm worried what he might do to us on Monday after this," Jerry said as Michael disappeared.

"Hey, I hadn't thought of that," Linda replied as she dug into her pocket for a handkerchief and used it to rub the worst of the mud off her face.

"If I so much as hear of him bullying again," Brian voice rose to a quiver, "I'll come with others from my unit and give him a week of hard drilling back at the camp! You two have done more and risked more in your short lives than a waster like him will ever do in a lifetime."

CHAPTER 4

"You wouldn't really hurt Michael, would you?" Linda questioned in concern as they walked back to the jeep.

"Oh no, not at all," Brian replied, "but I'd be happy to hand him over to our sergeant major for a couple of days of intensive parade drills. That should sort him out. In fact, in my humble opinion, Michael Meddlum should have had a good hiding or two when he was younger. He might not have ended up the big, lazy, interfering, self-opinionated lummox he is now. Anyway, he won't bother you two again."

"Will you really go and see his mother and the parents of the others?" Jerry enquired.

"Of course I will," Brian replied with a slight smile. "Hopefully such actions might dent the silly lad's stupid pride and ego. Anyway, let's not stand here chit-chatting. Jump in the jeep and I'll run you down to Ventnor. That's where you're heading, isn't it?"

As they travelled down the narrow track off the down and onto the road that led into town, Linda asked Brian how he came to be heading across the down just when they needed him.

"Well, I have some news. You see, I wanted to speak to you both so I went to see Mrs Griffiths. She told me that you had left to walk into Ventnor about half an hour before. I took a chance you had cut over the down and so drove up the track to find you. As I approached that wooded area I could see you all fighting and at first I thought some local youngsters were larking about, but as I got closer I could make out you two and realised you were in a bit of a fix."

"Huh," Jerry laughed. "A bit of a fix. You can say that again!"

"Okay, I will," responded Brian in a light-hearted tone. "You were both in a bit of a fix. So I stopped the jeep and jumped out. When I saw the lad holding you down, Linda, my blood boiled. You know, just as I got to you I heard you call out, 'Lord, save us,' and I nearly replied as I grabbed that lad, 'No, it's actually Brian, not God.' "

"But Brian, don't you see the Lord did answer my prayer?" Linda replied, smiling.

"He did?" Brian questioned as he slowed the jeep and crunched the gears at a junction in the town. "But it was me that came to your aid."

"Yes, it was you, but God sent you as He knew we would need your help." Then turning to Jerry in the back, she added, "Isn't God good?"

"Well, I like that," Brian laughed. "I come to your aid and fight off four attackers for you and God gets the credit!"

"Oh, Brian," Linda said, smiling at him. "You know I didn't mean it like that. God knew the best man to send at the right time and to the right place, so thank you too, Brian. You're great."

Brian parked the jeep near the seafront and turned round to look at Jerry. "How's the mouth? You took quite a knock on it by the look of all that blood."

"Just a split lip, I think," Jerry replied, running his tongue round his lips and tasting the blood that was still trickling from the cut.

"Here, let me have a little look at that."

"Oh, it's nothing."

"I'm the medic, remember."

"Okay, if you insist," Jerry reluctantly agreed.

After a good examination of Jerry's mouth, the medic pronounced the all clear. "Just a bad cut where you bit your lip, but thankfully no loose or broken teeth. Nothing that time cannot fix. Now what about you, young lady?" he asked, turning to Linda.

"Oh, I'm okay. Just a bit dirty and dusty from having my face pushed into the ground and a bit sore round my back where someone struck me, but I'll be fine."

"Good. Glad to hear it. You know, I could hardly believe seeing that Penhurst boy holding you face down into the ground. Talk about a coward. Why, if my father had ever found me hurting a girl, I'd have never sat down for a month!"

A little while later, the three friends were sitting on chairs outside a quaint little café in Ventnor, sipping from glasses of homemade lemonade.

"Brian," Linda enquired with a puzzled look on her face, "just why did you come to find us this morning?"

"Well, I have some bad news and some good news." He looked carefully around him to check no one was listening. The café was quiet and the people closest seemed to be fully engaged in their own conversation.

"Go on, give us the bad news first," Jerry responded, fully expecting Brian to inform them that there was no way they could get home.

Brian paused and looked away before going on. "Intelligence has informed those high up that your parents, Linda, have been arrested." Before Linda could let out a gasp of horror, he fixed his gaze on her. "But they are okay."

Linda turned pale. "But why…what…how…what else do you know?"

"I'll tell you all I know – just give me a chance! They have been arrested for supposedly helping Jerry's Uncle Fred and two French residents called Pierre and Nadia Le Blanc, relay secret plans of the Third Reich to London."

"But that's not true," Jerry exploded.

"Shh! Keep your voice down or else the whole café will want to listen in. We know it's not true, but they think you two are the French spies."

"What? We don't even look French, never mind speak much French!" Linda exclaimed.

"It's a case of mistaken identity by the Germans," Brian tried to explain. "Your parents Linda, knowing that you are safe here, have told the Gestapo that it was only you kids in the boat going to London to tell them about Hitler's supposed visit to Jersey. However the Germans are convinced that it was this French couple Pierre and Nadia who were in the boat. They think they are résistance workers. Pierre has risked his life and gone from France to Jersey to try to save your parents." Brian took a deep breath.

Jerry looked hard at him. "Keep going, Brian. What's the good news?"

"Well, it's that we need to get you home before the twentieth of September."

"Why before the twentieth of September?" asked Linda, some of the colour returning to her face.

"Because," Brian continued, "the Gestapo have said that if you return to Jersey, that will be proof that your parents and Uncle Fred are telling the truth. Linda's parents will be released, but it is likely that Pierre will be sent to prisoner of war camp."

"And if we don't...?" Jerry asked emphatically.

There was a silence.

"Come on, Brian, we want the truth; we are not afraid of it," Linda pleaded.

Brian looked straight at them both. "If you don't get home for the twentieth, it is likely that Pierre will be shot and that your parents, Linda, will go to prisoner of war camp somewhere in Germany."

With an expressionless face, Linda simply replied, "Thank you, Brian, for being honest with us. We will pray that we get back some way before the twentieth of September."

"Is anything being done to help us get back?" Jerry asked frantically.

"Yes, Jerry, as far as we know, plans are being worked on right now."

"Phew," Jerry let out a loud sigh in relief.

"Oh, my great aunt Sally," Brian cried out in alarm, breaking up the tense atmosphere. "I clean forgot about these." He fumbled through his jacket pocket and after pulling several faces he produced two scrunched-up pieces of paper. "Here," he said, "messages for you both from your parents."

"From our parents?" Jerry responded in a tone of unbelief. "How did you manage to get messages from our parents?"

"Do you two never stop asking questions?" The soldier chuckled. "Never mind how we got them, but we did. They are only short but they're for you."

After carefully unfolding each piece of paper, he handed each child their note.

Linda read hers out loud. " 'Linda, well done. Mum and Dad are proud of what you and Jerry did. Don't be disappointed it didn't all work out. We miss you terribly. Keep safe and out of mischief. All our love, Mum and Dad.' " Tears began to form in Linda's eyes. "So at least they know we made it and are safe," she said as she wiped her damp eyes. "When did they send this, Brian?"

"Just before they were arrested."

Jerry swallowed hard as he read, " 'Dear Jerry, so relieved you are safe. Hope England's okay. All well here. Missing you so much. Keep safe, son. Lots of love, Mum and Dad. P.S. Tell Linda not to tinker with any gear assemblies!' "

"What's that bit about gears mean?" Brian asked quizzically.

"Well, a couple of years ago I took the gear box on dad's car apart and couldn't put it together," Linda responded with a smile.

"Oh, I see. I forgot that you're a bit of a mechanic! Anyway, have a think about how you want to reply and write it down. One way or another, through some channel or other, we will arrange to get both of the messages delivered to your parents."

"But how can you do that, especially now Linda's parents have been arrested?" Jerry asked in surprise.

"Oh, we have ways and means in the army," Brian replied nonchalantly as he placed his empty glass of lemonade on the table. "Just write a couple of lines, no more than fifty words. Captain Cruickshank has promised to forward them to our contacts in the Channel Islands and they will get them to your parents."

"Oh, that's just great! Thank you so much," Jerry responded. He didn't dare ask any more questions. He felt Brian had told them all he was going to tell them for the day.

"Well, I think I should get you both back up to Mrs Griffiths'," Brian said, getting himself up from the seat in the café, totally forgetting that the children had intended spending the day in the town.

"Well, we haven't eaten our lunch yet or seen much of Ventnor." Jerry pulled a squashed brown paper bag out of his jacket pocket. "I forgot all about it with all the excitement of that combat with Michael Meddlum and then this news from home. Anyway, it looks like it's been ruined in the fight. It's all squished and squashed!"

"Yes, mine too," Linda added as another crushed paper bag was pulled rather unceremoniously out of her jacket. "Michael certainly messed up our lunch arrangements."

"Well, if there are no objections, then I will drive you both up to Mrs Griffiths' and she might be willing to let you both have something else to eat for lunch given the circumstances. And," he added, "maybe she will take pity on a hungry British soldier fighting for king and country. What do you think?" The jeep juddered into action.

Linda gave a little laugh. "I think with words like those, you will have Mrs Griffiths wrapped round your little finger."

CHAPTER 5

"My, oh my! Whatever happened to you two?" Mrs Griffiths exclaimed as the three walked into the large hallway of her home. "If I didn't know you two better, I'd say you'd have been in a fight, looking all dishevelled and dirty like that."

"Unfortunately, Mrs Griffiths, I have to inform you that I caught these two fighting about two hours ago on the far side of the down," Brian confessed with a wee twinkle in his eye.

"Oh, my dears!" Mrs Griffiths remarked, taking a deep breath.

"But don't worry, it was none of their doing and their chief tormentor will not be bothering them again."

"You didn't run into Michael, did you?" Mrs Griffiths said as she led them through into the lounge.

"They certainly did," Brian replied. "I think that Michael and his friends must have seen them as they came off the down onto the track that leads to Ventnor and waited for them by the woods."

"I think that might be true, because they just appeared out of nowhere," Jerry explained. "Then Michael said the down belonged to his family and we were not allowed on it, and that was it – they just attacked us."

"I always knew that Michael Meddlum was a no-good waste of space who would end up in prison one day," Mrs Griffiths said as she rolled her eyes in despair. "He'll deserve all he gets if he carries on like that."

"The problem," Brian confided, "is that he had others to help him do his dirty work. I pulled a lad called David Penhurst off Linda, but in my anger I forgot to get the other names. There were four of them, including Michael, and one was a girl."

"Ah, well, I can help you there," Mrs Griffiths explained. "If she was tall, with brown hair around shoulder-length and was rather strong-looking for a girl, that would be Rita Christie. The silly lass never knows when to keep away from trouble. She can be a good girl and should know better, but is just so easily led astray. Her parents will be most disappointed."

"Yes, that sounds like her," Brian confirmed as he looked again at Jerry's dirty clothes. "Listen, you two, why don't you get yourselves cleaned up while I fill Mrs Griffiths in on your other news, and then I'll go and have a little chat with both David's and Rita's parents." He turned to look at Mrs Griffiths. "Do you know where they live, Blodwyn?"

Brian filled Mrs Griffiths in on all the information he had passed on to the two children about Linda's parents' situation.

"How has Linda taken it? She's a very brave and plucky girl, you know."

"She seems okay for now and has taken it in her stride as I expected her to do, but just keep an eye on her."

"I'll do that all right."

"Well, let me go and sort out these bullies and time wasters, then I may pop back to check on our two brave ones before I head back to the barracks."

An hour later, Jerry and Linda, all cleaned up, reappeared downstairs, just before Brian turned up to check on them and report on his visits to the parents of the bullies. "I really don't think you will have any further trouble from David, Rita or the other boy, Alan Dobbins, in the future," he announced. "I have spoken to all their parents and they were pretty shocked to hear about what their children had been up to. David's parents were totally beside themselves with rage when I told them I had had to pull him off you, Linda. I certainly would not like to be in his shoes when he gets home!"

"Oh, poor boy," Mrs Griffiths whispered under her breath but loud enough for all to hear. "Mind you, I guess he deserves all that's coming to him. Anyway, let's not talk about those bullies any longer. It's too depressing. I think lunch is long overdue, so we'll call it high tea. I have made a salad full of good, healthy, home-grown vegetables and a little homemade cheese for us all, so let's sit down to eat."

At that moment, the doorbell rang with its characteristic ding-dong.

"Oh, my! I wonder who that could ever be," Mrs Griffiths said, rising from the table to answer the door. The others continued eating. Muffled voices could be heard in the hallway, then the door into the dining room opened and Mrs Griffiths stood there with a rather dishevelled individual. Everyone looked up from the table to see David Penhurst, looking very uncomfortable and embarrassed.

"This young man has come here as he has something to say to you," Mrs Griffiths announced as she gently reached up and placed a hand lightly on the boy's shoulder. "Go on, David."

"Well, er…" His voice died away as he looked down at the blue and gold carpet. "Well I…er…just came to say…em…er… that I'm very…sorry about this morning. I know you never could…but I hope at sometime you can forgive me. Er, I'm just sorry…I was…er…involved. Thank you."

A silence came upon them all until Brian spoke up. "I shouldn't think they could ever forgive you after you setting upon them and hitting Linda like you did," he said sharply.

"Oh, but we can forgive you," Linda replied.

"We can?" Jerry asked with a look of surprise on his face.

"Yes, we certainly can," Linda responded excitedly.

Brian looked at them in amazement. "You two are just unbelievable."

Linda explained, "Well, God has forgiven us and because David says he's sorry we can forgive him." Linda looked at Jerry. "Do you remember that list of verses in Uncle Fred's Bible that he had written out in the back on one of those blank pages? I'm sure there's one about forgiving others. Hang on, David, while I go and get it."

Linda skipped out of the room and everyone remained silent as she ran upstairs with the speed of an athlete. In no time, she reappeared back in the room with the precious little leather-bound book in her hand. "Here," she said, turning to the back of the book and flicking through a few pages. "Let's see...ah, yes, here it is. The third verse down. 'Be ye kind one to another, tenderhearted, forgiving one another, even as God for Christ's sake hath forgiven you.' It's in Ephesians chapter four, verse thirty-two."

Silence again reigned at the dinner table. "I guess that if it is in the Bible, we have to obey it," said Jerry, getting up and walking to where David still stood uncomfortably next to Mrs Griffiths. "David, forget it happened. We forgive you."

"I don't believe it!" Brian declared. "How will I ever be able to explain this back at base? Two kids who believe the Bible, actually follow what it says and forgive someone who two hours before was beating the living daylights out of them. Well, I never!"

"You either believe this book and obey it or you don't believe it and ignore its teachings at your peril," Linda continued with mounting confidence. "David, my dad back in Jersey always told me that it takes a lot of guts to own up, admit you're wrong and say sorry. I think you're very brave coming here to apologise, and as Jerry said, we forgive you totally."

"Really?" questioned the older boy, looking up for the first time and seeing Jerry's smiling face. "You mean you really forgive me for what I did along with Michael and Alan and Rita earlier?"

"Yes, we do, because God has already forgiven us much more than we can ever forgive you," Jerry tried to explain. "He forgave us all our sins. Anyway, why don't you stay and have some of Mrs Griffiths' homemade rhubarb crumble?"

"No, no, I just couldn't do that. I mean, I er...must go home, but," he added with determination, "I don't think I will ever want to be friends with Michael again."

Mrs Griffiths, feeling sorry for the boy who she knew must have had some courage to come and apologise, looked at Brian and said, "Would you be able to run him home?"

"Me?" Brian questioned. "But I have only just returned from his house after telling his parents all that went on this morning."

"Oh, no! Do my parents know about this morning?" David's face creased up as if in great pain.

"Yes, they do, and I would not at all like to be in your shoes when you walk in through that front door, young man," Brian said, pushing his chair away to stand up.

"Then that is all the more reason for you to run David home and explain to his parents that he has apologised to us. Tell them that we have forgiven him and he is not to be punished any further," Jerry rationalised with the air of someone who has just won the final battle.

"Well," added Mr Griffiths as he placed his cutlery together on his plate, "I guess there is no more to be said. David, you are forgiven and well done for coming to apologise. Jerry, Linda, you are most kind in forgiving David. Brian, you had better do as Blodwyn says to save David any more trouble when he gets home."

"Hmm. Well, that's me told," Brian said with a wry smile on his face. "Come on, young man, let's run you back to Wroxall. Hey, don't forget to keep some of that rhubarb crumble for me when I get back."

With that, both soldier and chastised but forgiven youth left the house, the young man still murmuring words of thanks about his apology being so gladly accepted.

"Well, that is something you don't see every day," Mrs Griffiths said when the two had left the house. "That was a very nice thing to do to that young man, to forgive him in the way you did."

"I think he was very brave to come here to apologise," Linda replied.

"Yes, but he could have been trying to lessen the trouble

he was in," Jerry pondered as he looked through the curtains to watch Brian and David drive away.

"Maybe, especially as he was the only one who gave his name to Brian. However, I think he was genuinely sorry for what he had done. I have said I have forgiven him and I mean what I said," Linda stated, "and I feel quite happy about it all."

CHAPTER 6

Jerry and Linda kept the news about Linda's parents to themselves and quietly hoped and prayed that very soon, some way, somehow, they would be on their way to Jersey. They had thirteen days to get back to the Island. They knew that if they travelled by boat they could make the journey in a day, and by plane in an hour, but they knew that it wasn't going to be as straightforward as that. They knew too that the powers that be would not allow them to do anything dangerous, even though they had arrived on the Isle of Wight in one piece in a little boat.

Brian and Cuthbert seemed confident that the navy had everything in hand, but they were reluctant to answer any questions so Linda and Jerry tried to wait patiently.

School helped to keep them busy. They both noticed that Michael kept well away from them for the next few days. They also observed that he seemed to be very much alone as others shunned him by keeping out of his way.

Just as they were finishing tea on Wednesday evening, the doorbell reverberated with its familiar chime. Mr Griffiths trudged down the hallway and opened the heavy oak door. The youngsters could hear the clipped tones and clear voice of the army captain that they had first met after being washed up on the island a couple of months previously. They both stood up from the table as Mr Griffiths showed Captain Cruickshank into the dining room.

"No need to stand on ceremony for me," the captain laughed as he pulled up a chair at the table.

"I'll go and brew another pot of hot tea," Mrs Griffiths announced before signalling to her husband that they should both leave the room.

"Well then, how are you getting along?" the captain enquired matter-of-factly. He twiddled his right ear between thumb and forefinger. "Everyone treating you well here?"

The children nodded.

"Good, good. Glad to hear it. Now then, I believe that Brian had a long meeting with you on Saturday?"

The two tried to smile. "That is certainly one way of putting it," Jerry replied. "It was more than a meeting. In fact, Brian turned up just when we needed him." He continued with a vivid explanation of the fight they had found themselves in.

"Aha. I see," the captain said, leaning back into the chair. "You can always trust the army to turn up just when required. Now then, I believe he told you about Linda's parents and the need to get you two home. Did he give you the messages from your parents?"

The children both nodded.

"Good, good and do you have any messages to send to them? If so, I'm here to collect them."

"Yes," replied Linda. "Mine's all written out upstairs."

"And what about you, Jerry?"

"Er...yes," Jerry replied as if unsure of himself. He was desperate to ask if the captain had any plans about getting them home, but lacked the courage. "It's not written down. I'll just tell you what I want to say."

"That's fine."

As Linda headed upstairs to collect her note, Mrs Griffiths' plump frame appeared in the doorway carrying a tray containing a big teapot, three cups and saucers and an array of buns and biscuits.

"Good gracious," the captain remarked. "I thought we were rationed and these sorts of dainties weren't available anymore."

"If you're careful and cautious and collect bits and pieces, you can make things stretch out a long way, Captain," Mrs Griffiths explained with a twinkle in her eye as she placed the tray on the table. "Anyway, these are all homemade and as I'm a reasonable cook I know just how to make stuff like flour and sugar stretch out a bit!"

"And," interjected Jerry mischievously, "Mrs Griffiths only brings out the top notch food and expensive crockery like this when there is a very important guest here."

"Away with you," the hostess said as she gave Jerry a playful clip round the ears. "You're too cheeky, you are."

Linda came back eagerly waving a piece of paper in front of her with various words crossed out, added in and written over. "Here's my note to mum and dad. 'Dear Mum and Dad. I'm fine and so is Jerry. We are being well looked after but can't wait to get back home to help you out. Something will work out soon. Trying to keep out of mischief. Missing you both. Take care and don't worry about us. All my love, Linda.' " She stopped and looked up at the captain. "I had so much else I wanted to say, but Brian said no more than fifty words. I've cut it down but it still comes to fifty-two. Is that okay?"

"Yes, it most certainly is, my dear." Captain Cruickshank took the piece of paper from Linda. "I will get this tidied up and sent to our intelligence boys who will arrange for the message to be delivered to your parents. Now, Jerry, what about you?"

"Well, I just want to say something similar to Linda," he admitted in an almost embarrassed manner. "How about 'Dear Mum and Dad. We made it safely and are fine. Glad Uncle Fred is okay. We are living on the Isle of Wight with Mr and Mrs Griffiths. They are very kind. Hope to be home soon. Love, Jerry.' How many words is that?"

The captain quickly counted up. "Forty, so that will do nicely. It's good to be brief. I'll get these sorted as soon as I can."

"But how will you get them to our parents, especially Linda's, now they've been arrested?" Jerry questioned.

"Now, don't you be worrying about that. Just leave it with us. We have ways of getting messages to people."

Jerry wanted to quiz him more, but Linda gave him such

a hard look he decided it was probably best just to leave it there.

Captain Cruickshank pushed his chair back from the table as if he was about to take his leave, then paused and turned to look at the children again. "Now, I need to speak to you about another very important thing. I know you both want to get back home to relieve Linda's parents from the predicament they are in. Sergeant Rennoldson, Corporal Oliver and myself have all made strong representations to our superiors on your behalf about this, however, you must realise just how dangerous that venture will be, crossing the Channel and taking you close to Jersey without coming under German gunfire. A plan has been suggested, which has the full backing of the War Cabinet."

Jerry and Linda looked at each other in surprise. Those in authority were certainly making a lot of effort to return them to Jersey.

"The plan," continued the captain, "is that you go so far on a Royal Navy frigate which is going out into the Channel on the eighteenth of September. It should be able to sail reasonably close to Jersey. From there, we may be able to transfer you onto its motor launch in the dark of night to meet up with a small boat out of Jersey. If that works out, once you arrive on Jersey and present yourselves to the German authorities, hopefully you should secure the release of Linda's parents and save Pierre Le Blanc from death. You must understand that you are on your own once you are in that little boat heading back to Jersey. I cannot force you to stay and remain safe here on the Isle of Wight. Amazingly, the powers that be have authorised my own commanding officer to assist you in every way required to return you both home. It is totally your choice."

As he finished, there was a silence that filled the dining room.

"There is no choice. We must head back home," Jerry said, breaking the silence. "After all, if God could protect us from that minefield we walked through at Freshwater, I am sure He can protect us from the dangers as we return home."

"And what about you?" the captain enquired tenderly as he turned to Linda. "I suppose with your parents in danger, your reply will be the same."

"Yes, Jerry is right. There is no choice. We go whatever the cost," she replied. "God will be with us."

"Once again, you both prove to be very brave young people." He stood up, placing a hand on each of their shoulders and said, "In case I am unable to see you both before you leave, may I wish you Godspeed on your journey home."

With that, he headed towards the door, then turned and said, "It has been a pleasure and an honour to have known you for the short time I have done so. Good night."

"Well, my dears," Mrs Griffiths enquired as she returned from letting the captain out. "What decision have you made? I do hope it is to stay as it will be much safer and you have really brightened up the lives of Geoff and I."

"I'm sorry," Linda replied, going to hug the older lady who had been so kind to them. "We need to try to get home for my parents and to save this man Pierre from being shot. Please don't worry. If God can bring us safely here, He can take us safely back as well if that is what He wants."

"I know you are right," their guardian sighed. "It's such a wicked, cruel war! You'll just have to promise to come back here to stay once the war is over and then I'll make you Welsh cakes and pies every day."

"I think that is a done deal," Jerry laughed, "but we could always take one or two with us on our trip back home, if you don't mind?"

"I'm sure I can manage that, young man. It will be the least that I can do for you two."

Just then, the phone rang and Mrs Griffiths trotted out to answer it. The two children started making their way up the long, wide staircase to their rooms when their hostess called them back.

"It's Sergeant Rennoldson on the phone. He says that he and Brian have a day off duty on Saturday. They would like to take you to Cowes for the day and he wants to know if you'd like that?"

"Oh yes, indeed," shrieked Linda. "That would be great fun! We need to make the most of the next ten days before we head for home."

"Tell him he has to find us a shop that sells real ice cream," Jerry chipped in with a big smile on his face.

"I think," Mrs Griffiths said, placing the speaker back to her ear and the main phone to her mouth, "that they are delighted with that idea, Cuthbert, and," she added, winking at the two youngsters who had come back down and were standing at the foot of the stairs, "it may well help to keep them out of any more mischief and fights!"

School seemed to really drag out as the two friends waited in anticipation for more details of the plans to get them home. They were pleased to have Saturday to look forward to. The only bright part in the week was when Mrs Turner asked them both to tell the pupils all about Jersey. Neither Linda nor Jerry were able to resist such an opportunity to boast about their island home and even the brooding form of Michael scowling at the back of the classroom did not put them off as they enthused about their beautiful island.

CHAPTER 7

Saturday morning dawned bright and sunny as Jerry and Linda bounced down the stairs for breakfast unexpectedly early. Mrs Griffiths was kneading some bread dough, still in her dressing gown and curlers. "Oh my, oh my," she cried with embarrassment. "Whatever are you two doing down at this hour? It's still not seven and I was just putting a little something special for you in the oven for breakfast. I wasn't expecting you down for another hour at least. Oh my!"

"Don't worry," Jerry laughed as he gazed curiously at the curlers adorning her head. "We won't tell anyone about your hairstyle. Your secret is safe with us. Unless, that is," he added with a cheeky grin, "Mrs Turner at school asks us to give a talk on the Isle of Wight and its unusual characters!"

Mrs Griffiths rolled her head back and roared with laughter. "You're getting more cheeky every day, young man," she scolded, "although it really is good fun having you two bright bobbins around the house...even if you do catch me in my curlers!"

"We are just going into the lounge to read Uncle Fred's Bible, so there's no rush for breakfast," Linda informed her. "And you did say that Cuthbert and Brian wouldn't be here until ten, so there's plenty of time."

The two friends wandered into the lounge. After opening the heavy lined curtains round the large bay window to allow the early morning September sunshine to flood in, they sat down together. Jerry thumbed through the rather battered-looking Bible that had been left in the boat by Uncle Fred when he had been captured by the Germans in Guernsey.

"Where shall we read today?" Linda asked Jerry as he opened the little leather book.

"I found some really interesting verses near the beginning of Matthew's Gospel the other night when I was reading through it. Let's read those." Then, thumbing through the pages, he finally found Matthew chapter five and commenced to read. " 'And seeing the multitudes, He went up into a mountain: and when He was set, His disciples came unto Him: And He opened His mouth, and taught them, saying, Blessed are the poor in spirit: for theirs is the kingdom of heaven.' "

"What do you think 'blessed' means?" Linda asked, interrupting him.

"Do you know, I wondered about that too, but look at the next page. My uncle has written 'Blessed equals happy,' so I guess it means happy."

"Look how many verses start with that word. Why, there are nine of them, so I guess that in this chapter the Lord Jesus must be speaking about the secret of happiness, don't you?"

"Um, I hadn't thought about it that way, but I guess you must be right."

Jerry read on and then stopped after turning over a page. "Hey, look at this verse that Uncle Fred has also underlined. 'But I say unto you, Love your enemies, bless them that curse you, do good to them that hate you, and pray for them which despitefully use you, and persecute you.' There's more writing from my uncle. It says 'Even the Germans.' How strange!"

"Jerry, do you think that maybe your uncle is saying that we have to obey those words and show kindness and love even to people like the Gestapo?"

"Well, I don't know," Jerry confessed honestly, "but they are our enemies and it does say we are to do good to them and pray for them."

"I don't mind praying for them," Linda replied, gazing at the underlined verse on the page, "but I'm not at all sure how I could do good to any Germans I may come across."

"Perhaps the Lord will show us that when the time comes," Jerry said thoughtfully as he looked again at the verses.

"Breakfast's ready!" Mrs Griffiths call came ringing from the kitchen, summoning the children. They got up and quickly made for the kitchen, out of which drifted the unmistakable smell of fresh bread. "Come along now, you two, and sit down. You can't go out to Cowes on empty stomachs."

"Are you going to Cowes?" her husband asked.

"I told you they were the other night, when Cuthbert phoned," his wife replied in an exasperated tone.

"Well, what did Cuthbert have to do with it?"

"He's taking them with Brian."

"Taking who?"

"Jerry and Linda, to Cowes. He phoned the other night to say he and Brian had a day off duty and to ask if Jerry and Linda wanted to visit Cowes with them," she explained, her patience stretched to almost breaking point.

"Oh, I see," Geoff replied, winking at the two across the table.

At ten o'clock sharp, the familiar ding-dong of the bell at the front door announced the arrival of their two soldier friends. Both young people rushed to answer it, swinging back the large oak and stained-glass inner door, before turning the big key in the lock of the large, solid outer door.

"Hello," chirped both soldiers almost together as their friends appeared. "How are you this fine sunny September morning?"

"Oh, we are great," Jerry answered with a beaming smile.

"They've been up since seven," Mr Griffiths called out down the hallway. "Caught Blodwyn in her curlers too."

"Oh, Geoff," his embarrassed wife scolded.

"Well, maybe we should have arrived earlier too," Brian laughed, looking at Mrs Griffiths.

"Away with you," she teased, "before I get my broomstick and chase you all along my garden path!"

The four ran in mock fun down the path and jumped into the open-top jeep parked on the road outside. In no time,

Brian had the engine started, and putting it into gear, roared off with a screech as Jerry and Linda waved from the rear in the direction of the rapidly-disappearing Mrs Griffiths.

"First stop," announced Cuthbert, "is a nice little place at Whippingham, right on the banks of the River Medina, where we can have a nice lemonade and just watch the world go by and forget about Adolf Hitler, Herman Goering, Joseph Goebbels and the rest of those nasty Nazis. You two can paddle in the edge of the river if you want. Then later we'll head into Cowes and see if we can get some lunch."

The journey only took about fifteen minutes before the jeep pulled sharply up outside a quaint little café on the banks of the river.

The two young people looked out in amazement across the river.

"It's so wide," Jerry said.

"We don't really have any rivers in Jersey, just the odd stream," Linda explained, "but this really is wide. Why, it is even wider than the Thames that we crossed with you in London when we first arrived."

"You're right," Cuthbert explained. "The Medina is very wide, probably because it's tidal. I guess that at this point it's over two hundred yards wide, but almost double that back there," he said, pointing upstream. "And the river isn't much more than four miles long!"

The four sat at a small, round, wooden table, looking down the river and sipping ice-cold lemonade. Occasionally, a small boat would pass along the river, travelling to or from Newport, the main town on the island. Further across, they could see two people in a small rowing boat who appeared to be fishing. Suddenly, one of them, who had his back to them, stood up and commenced to rock the boat vigorously. Even from the distance they were sitting, they could hear the voice of the other boy raised in fear.

"Michael, stop it! You'll capsize us...Michael!"

Brian was the first to realise who it was. "Oh no!" he exclaimed in alarm. "Not Michael Meddlum again. I had enough of him last week. And now what's he doing, the stupid boy?"

Almost before he had finished speaking, they watched as the bully suddenly seemed to lose his footing in the boat and fall. It seemed for an instant that he was going to recover, but then with a huge splash he disappeared over the side of the boat into the river.

All four watching with rapt attention from the safety of the shore burst into peals of laughter as they saw the big lad tumble into the water.

"Michael, you fool," the boy in the boat called out. "Get yourself back in."

"Serves the big oaf right," Brian said, grinning from ear to ear. "He deserves all that's coming to him."

Suddenly they heard the boy still in the boat call out, "Michael! Michael! Where are you?"

Jerry stood up and scanned the river, looking for the form of his previous tormenter to break water and appear alongside the boat.

"MICHAEL!" the now-frantic call of the boy left in the boat resounded across the water.

"Michael's in trouble," called Linda, running to the water's edge. "Come on, Jerry. We must save him."

"Now, just wait a minute," Cuthbert advised. "That river is wide and deep and cold."

"And Michael might drown unless someone does something," Linda called back as she pulled off her shoes and commenced to wade into the water, removing her small jacket as she did so.

"No, stop! That river's tidal and much too dangerous to swim in," Cuthbert called, running to grab Jerry.

"I'm coming too," cried Jerry as he threw his shoes to the side. He pushed Cuthbert away, ran into the water and dived in, then began to swim towards the boat that moments before Michael had left in such an undignified manner.

"Stop! We'll get a boat," Brian called, as he too splashed into the water's edge in a vain attempt to stop Jerry and Linda.

"That'll take too long," Jerry called as he stopped swimming and turned on his back to call to the two soldiers. "We need to get to him now."

Brian ran to the café and told them to get the emergency services, whilst Cuthbert made for a boat that was moored nearby. It was a small boat with a motor and not made for rowing. He tried to start the motor but nothing happened. As Brian ran towards him, someone else came running with a couple of oars. The two soldiers grabbed them with relief. The boat was too wide to row in a conventional manner so the men sat at opposite sides and began to frantically paddle towards the middle of the river.

After what seemed like an age, Jerry arrived at the boy in the boat first, who was by now frantic. "He just fell in," he wailed over and over as Jerry pulled himself up on the side of the boat.

"There he is," Linda called as she finally swam alongside, pointing about twenty yards down the river. "It looks like he's unconscious. Come on." Linda struck out once again downriver towards Michael.

"I think he hit his head on the oar," the boy said, trying to pull himself together as Jerry let go of the boat to follow Linda.

Jerry and Linda swam to the unconscious body that had now surfaced and was floating in a face down position.

"Turn him over," Jerry shouted as he finally reached the lifeless body.

"I'm trying to," Linda gasped, "but he's too heavy."

"Here, let's both try," Jerry said as he also tried to roll Michael onto his back and get his face out of the water. Finally, with a lot of effort, both children managed to turn the larger boy around. "Row down and help us," Jerry shouted for all he was worth to Michael's friend, who seemed to be sitting transfixed in the boat. "Help us," Jerry called again, even more frantically.

"We're coming," Brian called as he and Cuthbert paddled the boat as best they could across to where the three youngsters were struggling in the water.

Suddenly Michael gasped and regaining consciousness began to panic.

Not knowing where he was or what had happened, he started fighting Jerry and Linda. "I can't swim," he cried out in terror as he pushed both Linda and Jerry under the water in a futile attempt to stay afloat.

Jerry managed to get free, and coming to the surface called again, "Help!"

Realising what was happening, Brian dived over the side of the boat that was now nearing the three children. He swam to the struggling trio, and grabbing hold of Michael, started to pull him towards the boat that Cuthbert was still frantically trying to manoeuvre closer, using the one oar as a paddle.

"Stop struggling, Michael, or you'll drown us all," Brian shouted with all the force he could into the boy's ear. "Let me do the work and you'll be safe. If you struggle, we are all going to drown." Michael stopped struggling, and as he turned his head, Brian saw the look of fear in the boy's eyes.

"Help," Jerry called again, panic in his voice. "I can't see Linda!"

CHAPTER 8

Cuthbert reached over the side of the boat. He grabbed the back of Michael's jacket and helped heave him aboard.

"Thank you! Thank you!" Michael called out as he grabbed the sergeant's legs.

"Shut up and stay there," Cuthbert ordered.

"Help!" a voice called from further down the river. "Help!"

Cuthbert looked up to see Linda now struggling to keep her head above water about thirty yards away. He dived in over Brian, who had left the side of the boat to help Jerry. When Brian saw that Jerry was climbing into the boat occupied by Michael's friend, he immediately changed direction to swim behind his colleague towards Linda, who was trying to keep from drowning.

"Help!" she spluttered and disappeared under the water.

"We're coming," Cuthbert yelled as he dived under the water, his strong arms taking hold of her and pulling her up. Between them, they managed to drag her towards the boat where Michael still lay coughing and spluttering. On the shore they could hear the unmistakable bell of an ambulance as it arrived at the café where a few moments before they had been enjoying lemonade together.

As they got to the boat, another person swam out to them pulling a rope behind him. As he came closer, both soldiers could see that he was wearing a pale blue shirt.

"I'm a police officer," he gasped out. "Here, we'll tie this to the boat and my colleague will pull us all in." He undid a small rope that was tied around his waist, and swimming round to the front of the boat Brian and Cuthbert had used, he managed to tie the rope to the bow.

Meanwhile, Brian and Cuthbert carefully lifted Linda over the side and into the boat to join Michael sitting on its floor.

"I think if we all try getting in we'll likely as not capsize the thing," the policeman said as he held the side.

"I think you're right," Cuthbert replied, breathing heavily. "Let's just put our hand on to the side here and get pulled in with it."

Brian, grabbing hold of the opposite side to the policeman and Cuthbert, called across to Jerry, who was panting heavily in the other boat where the other boy still sat as if frozen in time, "Linda's safe. She's okay!"

Eventually, with a lot of pulling from a policeman on the shore and various customers from the café, the boat containing Michael and Linda reached the muddy side of the river with Brian, Cuthbert and the policeman clinging to its side.

Both soldiers collapsed with exhaustion onto the sandy shoreline as an ambulance man attended to Linda. She was coughing loudly and shivering uncontrollably. In the bottom of the boat, Michael Meddlum looked a very sorry state and hardly anyone was paying any attention to the one who had caused all the drama in the first place. His head ached, his lungs ached and his pride was crushed.

Jerry and the other boy, who he had discovered was called Russell, managed to row the boat they were in to shore. As they reached the shore, an older man came to meet Jerry, saying, "Man, you and that girlfriend of yours deserve a medal for what you both did today. Why, if it had not been for you, that clot would be dead by now." He pointed at Michael who was climbing gingerly out of the other boat.

Jerry, ignoring the man, ran first to see Linda and then, realising that she was being taken care of, went and sat down next to Michael. "I'm glad we were here to save you," he said tenderly. "I'll get one of the ambulance men to look at your head where you knocked yourself out."

"Thank you," Michael replied quietly and dejectedly.

"Is everyone okay?" Jerry heard Linda ask after a couple of minutes.

"Yes, we are, thank the Lord," Brian replied.

"Yes, we do need to thank the Lord, Brian," Linda said, still shivering more with shock than the cold.

The girl smiled as another ambulance arrived, and Jerry, along with Michael, was wrapped in warm blankets. "You know," she coughed as she was carried on a stretcher to the first ambulance, "we are not doing too well between us here, are we, Jerry?"

"What do you mean?"

"Well, when we first arrived, you ended up in hospital and now it looks like I'm going there too." She smiled weakly then coughed again.

"You'll be all right, Linda," Jerry said as he watched the door close.

"Do you want to travel with her?" an attendant enquired.

"Er, yes, but..." Jerry hesitated as he looked at the figure of Michael Meddlum sitting forlornly on the grass without a friend in the world. Looking at Brian who was explaining to a policeman what had taken place, he said, "Brian, will you go with Linda, please, in the ambulance? It's just, er...I'd like to stay here a bit longer." He motioned his head in the direction of Michael. "I think someone needs a friend."

"What's happened to your friend Russell?" Jerry asked Michael.

"I dunno. I s'pose he's gone home."

"Come with us and we'll follow Linda to the hospital in Brian's jeep."

Two hours later, at St. Mary's Hospital in Newport, Cuthbert, Brian, Linda, Jerry, a policeman and the cause of all the trouble, Michael, were dry, clean, warm and clothed as they waited to be checked over by a doctor.

"Well, Michael, I have never met you until today," Cuthbert remarked, "but I have heard about you and I confess that what I have heard has not been good!"

The young man sat in sullen silence, staring at some invisible point on the opposite wall.

"Whatever were you trying to do in the boat?" Cuthbert questioned in a kind but firm manner.

"Scare. My. Friend," Michael announced in a slow, stilted voice.

"Well, from what we saw, you certainly did that all right," Brian interrupted. "He was so scared he never came to help any of us. He just sat there watching and panicking like a great pudding!"

Michael changed his gaze from the wall to the floor.

"You do realise that your silly prank almost killed six people?" Cuthbert continued, still looking at the boy.

Michael raised his head and all of them could see that he looked very anxious about what had happened.

"Yes, you could have been responsible not only for your own death, but those of Linda, Jerry, Brian, Constable Rankin and myself."

As the seriousness of what might have happened sank in, Michael could contain his tears no longer and exploded in a torrent of sobs as he shook uncontrollably.

"But I didn't mean to," he wailed.

Linda moved across to comfort the distraught boy.

"I know you didn't," she said kindly. "And thankfully no major harm was done. Apart from a few cold people, wet clothes and my torn skirt, we are all fine and," she continued earnestly, "I think we all have God to thank for that!"

"But why...?" Michael's voice trailed away.

"Why what?" Linda questioned.

"Why did you come to save me, knowing how I had treated you last week?"

"Because we knew God wanted us to help you."

"How?"

"We were reading the Bible this morning before breakfast and we read a verse that said we had to love our enemies and do good to them, so that's just what we tried to do when we saw you in trouble in the river," Linda explained.

"But I don't understand."

"You won't," Jerry replied. "But that just seems to be how God works. He points something out to us in the Bible and expects us to do what it says."

"I don't believe the Bible," Michael confessed.

"That doesn't matter," Linda replied. "The fact is, whether you believe it or not, it's true! You just need to have trust in it and in the Lord Jesus. That then changes everything for you."

"You know," Cuthbert said, turning to his colleague, "I'm getting very worried about all this religion coming from these two children. It sort of makes me uncomfortable, but also makes me want to know more. Do you remember that bed and breakfast we all stayed at in London when they arrived? First it was Linda who told us she had trusted Jesus to save her, then, blow me down, Jerry goes and says the same a bit later. It's a right strange thing, I can tell you."

"I know what you mean," Brian replied. "I went to Sunday school, so I think I know a little of what they are talking about. They taught us there that to be in heaven you need to have your sins forgiven and trust Jesus as your Saviour. It amazes me how two youngsters, only just in their teens, can forgive someone for attacking them as I saw them do last week after the fight. Now today they risk their lives to rescue one of the other boys who attacked them and they say a verse in the Bible helped them do it. It is a strange thing!"

For the first time, Michael looked up and into the faces of first Linda and then Jerry before saying quietly, "Thank you for saving my life."

"I should think so too," Cuthbert interjected.

Ignoring Cuthbert, Michael asked again, "Why have you been so good to me?"

"Simply because Linda and I are Christians and therefore realise how important it is to forgive someone when they have done wrong."

"Just as God has forgiven us our sins because the Lord Jesus died on the cross, so that helps us to forgive you," Linda answered with a reassuring smile.

"Linda De La Haye?" a nurse called.

"That's me," Linda replied, standing to her feet and realising for the first time since arriving in hospital that she was still cold.

"Come this way, please," the nurse said with a wave of the hand. "Doctor will see you now."

"I'm glad to report that none of you seem to be any the worse for wear after your ordeal this morning," the doctor announced after seeing all the casualties. "Michael just had a bad knock to his head and may feel fuzzy over the next forty-eight hours or so and could have a headache for the rest of today. Linda just needs to keep warm and hopefully she will avoid a cold, or worse, influenza, although she did get very chilled in that water. The rest of you thankfully seem to be okay and you can all be discharged."

"Well, that is a mercy," Brian said to the policeman who was sitting alongside him dressed in a white doctor's coat and with a large white towel still around his neck and shoulders.

"I think the inspector at Cowes will require a report," the policeman said as he stood up. "I believe my colleague has all your details but if you would all pop round later today to the police station it would be appreciated."

"Oh no," groaned Michael. "Now I'll be in more trouble."

"No, you won't," Jerry replied. "I think you have well and truly learned your lesson over these past two weekends, that it's not good to bully people. I am sure you will not be doing it again."

"No...n-n-no...no, I won't. I p-p-promise," the boy replied, still with a frightened look upon his face. "I'll never do it again but I cannot understand why you saved my life today. I'd have been glad if you had died."

"Look, let's go home and get changed, get some food and then give the statement down at the police station. After that, we can talk some more. Is that a deal?"

CHAPTER 9

Michael had managed to borrow a pair of shorts and a belt from Mr Griffiths and a top from Jerry. He looked a bit of a sight, but surprisingly he didn't seem to care. The soldiers returned to their barracks where they discovered that the only clean clothes they had were their spare uniforms. After they were all clad in dry clothes, they made their way to the small police station in Newport to give an account of the happenings that morning on the River Medina.

Once again, Michael had felt awful at being branded the 'bad guy' by both Cuthbert and Brian, even though he knew that was exactly what he was. The young man was aware that he owed a lot to Linda and Jerry, who had both defended him, even though his actions had nearly led to the deaths of several people.

"Well, now that's over," announced Cuthbert matter-of-factly, "what do you say to a trip to West Cowes and to one of the few shops that still sells ice cream on the island?"

"Yes, sir," enthused Jerry, licking his lips. "Sounds good to me!"

Within no time at all, Brian was driving, with the three children sitting across the back of the jeep, at high speed out of Newport and along the west banks of the River Medina. As he slowed to enter the town of West Cowes, Cuthbert turned to the children.

"Cowes is a funny town. It's built on either side of the mouth of the river, so we are entering West Cowes and across that side," he said, pointing to buildings over the river, "is East Cowes. In fact, there is one of those nonsense rhymes about the two parts. 'The two great Cowes that in loud thunder roar, this on the eastern, that the western shore.' "

"Hey, I never heard that before," Michael said, speaking for the first time.

"Possibly because Cuthbert just made it up," Linda laughed.

"No, I didn't," the sergeant protested. "It was written in the last century by some American chap."

"Well, I agree with Linda," Brian smiled as he slowed the jeep to a stop. "It sounds like you made it up! Anyway, who wants to see Cowes' famous floating bridge?"

"Whatever is a floating bridge?" Linda asked, a look of disbelief crossing her face.

Brian moved the vehicle round a corner to where the children could see a boat-like craft moving across the river. It had what seemed like a long road protruding out of each end and two giant trumpet-like horns sticking up into the air at either side.

"That is what is known as a floating bridge," Brian continued as they watched the craft coming closer to them. "It is actually a ferry that is pulled by two enormous chains across the river. Vehicles can drive on and be taken across the water between East and West Cowes."

"That is amazing," Jerry responded as he watched the ferry pull up not far in front of them. "We never had anything like that in Jersey."

"We don't have any rivers in Jersey," Linda chuckled, "so we wouldn't need one of those."

"It is rather unique," Cuthbert remarked, "but I thought we were going for ice cream, Brian, not a sightseeing tour of river crossings. I have had more than my fill of rivers for one day."

He glanced at Michael, who, once again embarrassed, looked down at the floor of the jeep and mumbled, "I'm sorry."

"I know you are, young man. I know you are," Cuthbert responded as he reached across into the rear of the jeep and ruffled Michael's tousled hair. "I think today has been a big turning point in your life."

"I'm never going to hurt nobody ever again," the chastened lad answered. "It gets you into more trouble than it's worth!"

Ten minutes later, as the bright afternoon sun shone down upon them, casting short shadows, the two soldiers and their charges sat happily licking ice cream cones as if they would never taste them again. "And to think that there were dozens of shops selling ice cream in every seaside town around the country before the war started," Cuthbert complained. "Now it is hard to find one anywhere with all this rationing."

"Well, there was still ice cream in Jersey when we left," Linda replied, taking another long lick of her cone that was diminishing at a fast rate. "And ours was much creamier than this!"

"Oh, thank you very much," said Cuthbert mockingly. "I'll have what's left of your cone, if you don't mind – that cost me a penny!"

"No, you won't," Linda replied, enjoying another lick.

"It's just that our cows are much creamier than yours," Jerry said.

"I thought Jersey cows were brown, not cream," Brian added, entering the banter.

"You know exactly what I mean," Jerry replied with a big grin on his face. He tried to explain himself. "It's just that the milk we get from our Jersey cows is much richer and yellower than the milk that the cows here produce. My mum saves the cream, adds salt and shakes it very vigorously for ages to produce homemade butter. Then I love to drink the leftover liquid called buttermilk."

"Ugh! It is totally disgusting," Linda replied, pulling a face to show her obvious disapproval. "It tastes just like saltwater gone bad."

"Um, I have always wondered what rotten saltwater tasted like," Brian teased, giving Linda a playful grin.

Just then, a large black staff car pulled up on the road in front of the seats where the five friends were chatting. Out stepped Captain Cruikshank, and the two soldiers immediately stood up and came to attention.

"At ease," he responded jovially, then looking more intently at them he enquired, "Whatever are you two doing in uniform? I thought today was your day off?"

"Er, yes, sir. It was, sir, but you see, sir…Well, it's like this, sir…" Cuthbert mumbled, wondering how to explain the events of earlier in the day.

"What he's trying to say, sir," Brian helpfully explained, "is that…Well, it was just that we sort of…Well, you see, sir…"

"What they are trying to say," Michael interrupted, "is that I was being very stupid on the river this morning and nearly got all of us drowned!"

The captain stood looking at the two soldiers and three children in stupefied silence.

"Well," he eventually said, "it looks as if no harm came to any of you apart from a few wet clothes, I expect, so no real damage done." He looked directly at Michael and continued in a severe tone, "I hope that you, young man, have learned your lesson."

"Yes, sir. I have, sir," he answered, looking at Jerry and Linda for encouragement.

"How can we help you, sir?" Cuthbert enquired cautiously, surprised that Captain Cruickshank had taken time to look them out. "Have the Germans commenced the invasion?"

"No, nothing like that," his commanding officer responded with a smile and then a pause to clear his throat. "Ugh, um, it's just that I have…" He paused as he looked at Michael. "Perhaps you'd like to take this young man for a walk?" the captain suggested to his two soldiers.

"Oh right, sir. Yes, sir. Of course, sir," Brian said, suddenly guessing that the captain wanted to talk to the children alone.

"I really don't think you have anything to worry about with Michael," Jerry said quickly as Brian made to remove him from the group. "I'm pretty sure that he won't spill the beans about anything you say after all he's been through these past few days."

"Well, I'm not sure," Captain Cruickshank countered, pondering his dilemma.

"I won't say anything. Honest!" Michael added, hoping for once that someone would actually trust him.

"Okay," the captain replied, still looking a little unsure of his decision. He paused before beginning again. "There has been a change of plan."

Linda looked at him frantically. "What? Are they not taking us home?"

"It's okay. You are still going home. In fact, this is a much safer plan and has the blessing of the prime minister himself."

"What? Winston Churchill? Why should he care about us when he has a whole army, air force and navy to look after?" Jerry questioned.

"You would be surprised, my young man, who the prime minister is interested in!"

Jerry began to wonder if there was more to the arrest of Linda's parents and Pierre Le Blanc than anybody was ever going to tell them.

Captain Cruickshank continued, "Hopefully this will be a much safer way to get you home. I have now been given word by navy intelligence that they can arrange a submarine to sail close to Jersey in the near future . You two are to join it with the hope of allowing you both to be put ashore by rubber dingy on the North Coast cliffs. A submarine is a much safer option and can get you closer to the cliffs where the Island is least defended. The crew will hopefully be able to paddle you in under the cliffs and then it's up to you to find the best way up them. Do you think you could manage that?"

"If we are back in Jersey, we can manage anything," Jerry responded confidently.

"But please remember there are still many dangers, even going by submarine, and we cannot guarantee that you arrive home safely. However, we will do the very best we can to eliminate any dangers which there might be."

"Does that mean we will have to go under the sea in a submarine to get there?" Linda questioned as a look of concern crossed her face.

"Yes, it does, Linda," the captain replied matter-of-factly. "You will dive under water as you near Alderney and remain underwater until you surface around one mile from the north coast of your island."

"I wish I could go in a submarine," Michael interrupted. "I have always wanted to go under the water in a submarine."

"Well, I'm afraid that we will not allow that at all," the captain replied quickly, fearing that Linda and Jerry may somehow try to twist his arm on behalf of their newfound friend. "It would be totally out of the question. The Admiralty in Whitehall are not at all happy about two children travelling on board one of their submarines. They only relented when it was put to them how brave you had both been and because of the danger your parents are in. As Mr Churchill has approved the idea, there is no one who would dare to refuse him."

"I'm going to join the navy when I'm old enough," Michael enthused, "then I'll be able to travel in a submarine and sink German ships!"

"Well, that's good to know, my boy," the captain responded enthusiastically. "The more we have fighting the Germans, the sooner this terrible war will be over." Then turning back to Jerry and Linda, he said, "If you are still sure you want to go, you will be collected on Monday morning and taken to the mainland. You will be in Portsmouth by Monday evening. Tuesday, you will undergo some basic training and then you will most probably sail on Wednesday morning to rendezvous north of Jersey around midnight. Then, if all goes to plan, the submarine will surface and you will be taken by dingy to the base of the cliffs whilst the submarine submerges to stay out of sight. You will be dropped off where you can scramble up the cliffs and from there, I'm afraid, you will be on your own with regards to getting home and taking yourselves to the Gestapo headquarters. Hopefully they will release your parents. There are no guarantees of anything, but I would say if the prime minister has approved it, they are fairly sure your parents will be released."

"That's okay. We're going, aren't we, Jerry, however small the chances and however great the dangers?"

"Absolutely," Jerry agreed. "We will do whatever we can."

"We will get there before the twentieth, won't we?" Linda asked anxiously.

"That's the plan. I'll take my leave of you for now," the captain added, "as I still have a few loose ends to tie up. You enjoy yourselves and no more adventures until Wednesday."

"We won't," Linda promised with a smile as she watched Captain Cruickshank turn on his heels and stride purposefully back to his car.

"That seems a much better and safer plan to me than the frigate idea," Cuthbert commented. "I know that you managed to escape from Jersey, but to ask someone else to do what you did, pick you up and then return you in safety is undoubtedly asking for trouble. No, I think our captain and those up in London have come up with a much better and safer plan to get you both home."

"I hope everything goes okay and we get there before the twentieth," Linda added, a concerned frown crossing her usually cheerful countenance.

"Oh," said Brian, as he watched his superior being driven away at speed, "I guess that we will miss you two once Monday comes around. Cuthbert and I have kinda got used to having you around. It's been fun getting to know you both."

"Why, thank you, Brian," Jerry chipped in cheekily. "It's nice to know we will be missed!"

The trip back to Godshill in the open top jeep seemed much slower than usual. It was as if Brian was trying to savour the last precious few moments that he and Cuthbert expected they would share with their two young friends. They had been with them through quite a bit since their arrival on the Isle of Wight in July. Brian's usual speed and reckless throwing of the vehicle into every corner at full power, driving which had made Jerry sick the first time he had ridden as Brian's passenger, was missing. It was a comparatively smooth ride home and the five occupants of the jeep were unusually quiet, lost in their own thoughts of what the future might hold. Brian drove past Mrs Griffiths' front door and out of the village, heading in the direction of Michael's house.

"Are you going to tell my mum about this morning?" Michael questioned as Brian brought the jeep to a stuttering stop outside a red brick, semi-detached cottage that looked as if it had seen better days.

"No, I am not," Brian replied, smiling at the big lad for the first time. "I really believe that this morning's accident will be the means of you sorting yourself out, changing your ways and becoming the nice, useful young man I believe is hiding somewhere under the surface. If that's the case, for the rest of your life you will have these two young people to thank, and if you are going to turn over a new leaf, what good will it be if I go reporting you to your mum again? If the police decide to investigate things further, then they may be round to see you and your mother."

"Oh no," Michael groaned. "Do you think they will?"

"I don't think so," butted in Cuthbert from the front passenger seat as he turned round to look Michael straight in the eye. "I told them that you had well and truly learned your lesson and that the case was closed. I really don't think they'll come calling. Don't worry."

"Thank you. Oh, thank you!" Michael said as a huge smile of relief swept over his face.

"However," Brian interjected as a smile played on the corner of his mouth, "before the end of this war, many soldiers are going die in the fighting and if I'm one of them and I find out you have returned to your old ways of bullying and nastiness, I will personally come back and haunt you until you are too scared to walk out of your front door!"

"Don't worry, I really have learned my lesson today. Thank you for helping me," Michael said, looking at Linda and Jerry. "I owe you both a lot."

CHAPTER 10

The next morning Jerry and Linda bounced down the stairs of the Griffiths' house with more enthusiasm than usual. They were excited at the thought of heading home. As they bounded into the kitchen, they stopped in their tracks as they caught Mrs Griffiths dabbing her eyes with the corner of her apron. As soon as she saw them, she dropped her apron and busied herself around the cooker and the sink, hardly looking in their direction.

"Are you okay?" Linda asked kindly as she watched the rotund woman breezing around the kitchen without seemingly doing anything.

The older lady stopped her pretence at being busy and sat down heavily on one of the strong wooden chairs that were placed around her kitchen table. "No, I'm not okay, if the truth be known," she replied, once again dabbing her moist eyes with her apron. "I'm just thinking how dull the place is going to be without you two when you leave tomorrow." Then standing up and pressing her apron against her sides as if trying to rid it of some creases, she added, "Oh, don't you mind me. I'm just a silly old woman who has become very fond of some other people's children and selfishly wanted them to stay here for the duration of the war. I'm sorry. I just woke up this morning full of self pity at the thought of losing you two, instead of thinking how much you need to try to get back to Jersey. Don't mind me at all."

With that, Mrs Griffiths continued to bustle, flap, fiddle and fuss until Linda told her to sit down whilst she took over stirring the porridge that was bubbling and thickening on the large range cooker that seemed to take up one whole side of the kitchen.

"Oh, dear me," the two youngsters' guardian continued to babble as she took a seat once again. "I just can't seem to get my head round anything this morning. I'm all of a dither."

"Well, don't you worry about a thing," Linda said as she continued to stir the bubbling pan of porridge on the stove. "We will be just as sad to leave you tomorrow as you will be to see us go."

Jerry chirped in in agreement, "We will miss you terribly too but hopefully once this war is over, not only can we return and visit you here, you could come and visit us in Jersey."

"Well, that's real nice of you," Mrs Griffiths replied in her Welsh accent. "I'll look forward to that."

"Anyway," Jerry enthused as a twinkle came into his eye, "I just cannot wait to tell Mum and Dad that a lady called Blodwyn looked after us!"

"Be off with you, you cheeky monkey!" Mrs Griffiths retorted as she grabbed a towel and flicked it playfully in Jerry's direction.

As they were all tucking into porridge, Linda asked, "Can we go to the church with the thatched roof, near where we landed, for their service this morning?"

Mr Griffiths looked up from his porridge bowl towards Linda. "But that's St. Agnes Church. It's on the other side of the island, on the road up from Freshwater Bay to Freshwater village. Can't you go to one of the nearer churches?"

"Well, we could," Linda replied after slurping her last spoonful of porridge, "but that one looked kind of quaint when we passed it a couple of weeks ago and it's the only church that I have seen on the Isle of Wight that has a Bible verse posted outside it."

"We all just call it the 'thatched church'," Mrs Griffiths added.

"It would be nice to spend our last Sunday on the island in such an unusual church," said Jerry. "Especially one that's thatched and is just up from where we landed that night in the bay."

"Oh, all right," Mr Griffiths relented as he wiped his mouth with a napkin. "I'll get the car out and we will all drive over there for their morning service."

"Hooray," both children responded in unison. "Thank you so much."

It was an hour later that Mr Griffiths parked his big smart Humber Pullman in front of his house and tooted the deep-sounding horn to hurry everyone along.

As both children raced down the stairs, they stopped and stared at Mrs Griffiths. She was looking into the hallway mirror, trying to place the biggest hat either of them had ever seen, upon her head.

"Wow," Linda breathed in sheer admiration of the huge hat that now adorned the head of her host. "That's some hat."

The older woman blushed as she tried to tuck a loose hair below its wide brim. "Well," she answered, "we don't go to church too often and I thought I'd sort of go all posh-like." She smiled in slight embarrassment. "And our Geoff has his car out all ready to go. It's a rare thing for him to take that car anywhere, especially with a war on and petrol rationing. He's very proud of it, he is."

The three walked down the stone path that led from the house to the road. Jerry and Linda climbed into the rear of the large black car and settled into the big, comfortable leather upholstery whilst Mrs Griffiths struggled to get into the front passenger seat without dislodging her oversized hat. Eventually all were safely aboard. Mr Griffiths cranked the gear stick into place and the car pulled off slowly with a deep roar.

Linda and Jerry contented themselves with looking out of the windows as the car gently sped through the slightly undulating landscape across the island. Suddenly Mrs Griffiths let out a cry of consternation. "Geoff, those trousers don't match your jacket!"

"I know," he countered as he continued to manoeuvre the car along narrow country lanes. "I put my blazer on."

"But, Geoff, we are going to church. Everyone there will be dressed properly and you will be there in just your blazer and a pair of unmatched trousers. You should have put your blue suit on."

"Which blue suit?"

"The navy one you bought in Cardiff."

"That old suit? Why, it's ancient. It must be at least fifteen years old. No, no! I'll be much more comfortable in this jacket than that old suit."

"Yes, but everyone will be looking at you, wondering what this pauper is doing in their pews," then turning to the children in the back, she added, "won't they?"

Both Jerry and Linda could hardly contain themselves as they listened to their conversation from the rear of the car.

"Well, I think that jacket looks very smart," Jerry answered, trying to stick up for his host.

"Um, you would, Jerry. You're a boy! Linda, tell him he can't worship God dressed like that."

"Er, well," Linda spluttered, both stalling for time and trying to suppress a fit of the giggles. "Well, it's not too bad. I mean, he has a tie on so I wouldn't worry too much if I were you."

"But everyone dresses up to go to church," Mrs Griffiths continued, "and he looks such a scruff."

"No one will notice. They will all be looking at that big hat of yours," Jerry added cheekily.

"Oh, you...really...well," Mrs Griffiths mumbled. "Well, when I was a lass about your age, we had a revival up in the valleys. Everyone started going back to the churches and listening to preachers preaching, and, boy, they thundered out the message with *hwyl*, they did."

"What was that word you used?" Linda asked as the car swung round the bend at Freshwater Bay and commenced its final climb to the thatched church.

"Hwyl. Pronounced 'hoil' but spelt h-w-y-l," Mrs Griffiths explained, spelling out each letter. "It means to have energy, to be powerful and have a bit of go about you."

"Well, we all need a bit of 'go' about us now as it's nearly time for the service to begin," Mr Griffiths butted in.

"Well, I was just about to say, back in the olden days everyone went to church in their best clothes, suits and hats."

"Oh, come on and stop worrying about my jacket," her husband grumbled impatiently as he held the door open to allow his wife out.

The four entered the small porch area and went through the large oak doors. Just as they entered, the congregation rose and commenced to sing.

> *Oh God, our help in ages past,*
> *Our hope for years to come,*
> *Our shelter from the stormy blast,*
> *And our eternal home.*

As the congregation continued to sing the hymn, the four visitors made their way down the aisle of the church until they found seats right at the front, facing sideways to the preacher. Mr Griffiths filed in, followed by Jerry, Mrs Griffiths and finally Linda. They all stood as the last verse died away.

> *Oh God, our help in ages past,*
> *Our hope for years to come,*
> *Be Thou our guide while troubles last,*
> *And our eternal home.*

At the end of the singing of the hymn, everyone sat down while the preacher remained standing and commenced to pray. When he had finished praying, he announced his text from the Bible. "Today I would like to read from John's Gospel chapter fourteen, verses one and six. 'Let not your heart be troubled: ye believe in God, believe also in Me. Jesus saith unto him, I am the way, the truth, and the life: no man cometh unto the Father, but by Me.' "

"Hey!" Jerry, in excitement, suddenly called out in a rather loud whisper as he leaned across Mrs Griffiths to Linda. "Those are our verses, Linda! Those are the ones Uncle Fred left for us in the boat."

It seemed as if the whole congregation turned to look at Jerry. Suddenly becoming aware of those staring at him, he stopped whispering in such an excited manner. His face was red with embarrassment. He looked up towards the preacher who smiled kindly at him but continued calmly with his message for the day.

Sitting next to him, Mrs Griffiths died a thousand deaths of embarrassment as she quickly adjusted her hat to hide her face from the unpleasant stares of the people still looking in Jerry's direction.

Mr Griffiths bowed his head and covered his eyes as if in prayer, whilst Linda tried hard to suppress a fit of the giggles, both at her friend's outburst and Mr and Mrs Griffiths' obvious discomfort.

They heard very little of the rest of the message that morning, but pricked up their ears when they heard that following the service there would be a Sunday school. Jerry and Linda looked at each other and smiled, hoping that Mr and Mrs Griffiths would let them stay.

As they all filed out of the church, the preacher stood in the porch to shake the hand of every person who had attended his service. Jerry was last out of the building, and as he shook the preacher's hand, he mumbled an embarrassed apology for his loud whisper. The preacher stopped him and said, "Am I right in thinking that you are the boy that came across from Jersey in a small boat with some important information for the government?"

"Yes, and Linda too," he replied, rather sheepishly looking in Linda's direction.

"Is your name Jeremy?" asked the preacher.

"Almost. It's Jerry," he answered politely.

"Well, Jerry, would you and Linda like to join us for Sunday school? I would love to hear more of your story. From the snippets I've heard, it sounds fascinating."

"I'm sure Linda would like to, but I will have to check with Mr and Mrs Griffiths. They brought us."

"That's fine. You go and do that and if they allow you, we'll be starting in about fifteen minutes in the side room."

After getting permission from their guardians, Jerry and Linda found themselves seated in a small side room with Mr and Mrs Griffiths sitting politely, if not rather awkwardly, at the back. Mrs Griffiths' large hat seemed to be giving her quite a lot of trouble as she kept fidgeting with it.

The preacher began the Sunday school with warm words of welcome and a short prayer. He then smiled across at Jerry, and began, "There is a young man here today who has a very exciting and very heroic story. He is now going to tell you about his and his friend Linda's experiences."

Jerry gingerly stood up and found himself standing before a group of children, once again having to relate their story. This time he felt no fear, and in complete confidence he began, knowing this was quite a different group of children to those they had told their story to at the school.

CHAPTER 11

"Now then, young man. May I ask you some questions?"

Jerry nodded slowly as he glanced at the rows of slightly upturned faces looking expectantly at him.

"Excellent," the preacher enthused. "Now, would you tell these boys and girls what your name is?"

"Jerry Le Godel."

"That is not a name from this island, is it?"

"No, I'm from Jersey. I arrived here in July with Linda."

"You landed in the bay down the road from here, didn't you?"

"Yes, that's right, we did, in the middle of a storm."

"Would you tell us how you were kept from drowning and from being blown up by mines on that beach?"

"Well, God promised us before we left Jersey that He would protect us through the waters and the fire, and He did."

"How did God promise you that?"

"Oh, my Uncle Fred read it out of his Bible the afternoon before we left Jersey."

"So you believe that God can speak from this book, the Bible?"

"Yes, sir, I do, because I believe that it is God's Word and so does Linda," Jerry added, pointing at Linda who was listening attentively to the answers Jerry was giving.

"Great! I too believe that this precious book is God's never-changing Word and I hope that all the boys and girls here today realise and understand its importance too. Now, Jerry, why did you come all the way to the Isle of Wight from occupied Jersey?"

"Because Linda and I had heard that Adolf Hitler was planning to visit Jersey and we thought that we needed to tell people in England about this visit."

"Why did you believe that you needed to tell those in England about Hitler's planned visit to Jersey?"

"It was because we thought that the Allied forces might be able to mount an attack on him...I mean, an assassination attempt. You see, the Germans invaded our island. Last year they bombed St. Helier. Some people were injured and killed, though it was worse in Guernsey. For the rest of us, life changed."

"How did life change, Jerry? Was it really bad?"

"Well, we were issued with special identity cards that we had to carry with us everywhere. We also had to be in the house by a certain time each night and not leave before a certain time each morning. There were German troops everywhere you went. They also took most of the islanders' cars and almost completely emptied the shops, buying things for their families that they obviously couldn't get back home. If they liked someone's house they just ordered the owner out and took it over. Then we had our currency changed from the British Pound to the German Reichsmark. When we learned that Hitler was planning on coming to the Island, we thought that, whether he flew or sailed in, he could be attacked, and if he died Jersey would be free and the war would be over."

"So tell us about what happened on your sea adventure from Jersey?"

"Before we left we discovered that someone had stolen some of our petrol for the outboard motor, so we had to stop in Guernsey to get some. That's where Uncle Fred was captured by the Germans and we had to come on alone."

"Tell us a bit more about your Uncle Fred."

"He is a Christian, but before he became a Christian he was a wild-living sailor. Then one day, during the first war, he was in Belfast and he heard someone preaching about the love of God. He got saved by trusting in the Lord Jesus as his Saviour. That changed his life completely.

"When Uncle Fred was caught by the Germans on our way up here, Linda and I were very frightened, but we found those verses you read at the start of this morning's service.

Uncle Fred had placed a bookmark in that page of his Bible, and he had also underlined those verses, I guess so that we could find them. We thought they were some sort of code from God – that He was telling us that we were not to worry and everything would work out in the end. The more we read and thought about those verses, the more we realised that God had sent His Son and we needed to believe in Him because He is the way to heaven."

"You discovered all that in a little boat coming up the English Channel?"

"Yes, but it wasn't until after we arrived in England that we both decided we just had to trust the Lord Jesus as our Saviour. We knew He was a God worth trusting."

"So, Jerry, let me ask you – are you and Linda going to heaven?"

"Yes, absolutely!"

"Because you trusted the Lord Jesus as Saviour?"

"Yes. We trusted Him because He died for us."

"Jerry, that is the best news that I have heard in a long while. Thank you so much for telling your story to these boys and girls. Would you also tell us a bit more about your journey across the sea and on to London? Didn't you get to visit Westminster?"

As briefly as he could, Jerry told the children of the Sunday school how he and Linda had negotiated the English Channel and been thrown up on Freshwater Bay in a storm and then how God had kept them safe as they crossed the mined beach.

As Jerry took his seat again next to Linda, he noticed Mrs Griffiths wiping away the tears from her eyes, the big hat getting in the way once again. The boys and girls still sat there spellbound.

The preacher stood and flicked over the song sheets until he found the chorus 'I am the way, the truth and the life'. "We are going to sing this chorus before we leave," he announced.

The children in the Sunday school stood up and started to sing.

I am the way, the truth and the life, that's what Jesus said.

I am the way, the truth and the life, that's what Jesus said.

Without the way there is no going,

Without the truth there is no knowing,

Without the life there is no growing.

I am the way, the truth and the life, that's what Jesus said.

The boys and girls, more lustily than ever, sang out the words of the song before the preacher finished off their lesson for the day.

"Children, if we are ever going to arrive in heaven, it will only be when we realise that we cannot get there on our own because our sin will keep us out forever. We needed someone to come who was able to remove our sin and make heaven available to us. Just as Jerry and Linda came to realise, it is only the Lord Jesus who can make us fit for heaven, if we are prepared to trust Him as our Saviour from sin."

Sunday school was over and the preacher thanked Jerry for sharing about his salvation and their amazing adventure.

"Well done, son. Our nation needs more people like you and Linda. You have had one great adventure, but the biggest and best is still before you and that is walking with God. Keep living for Him!" He quoted a verse from the Bible for them, " 'Trust in the Lord with all thine heart; and lean not unto thine own understanding. In all thy ways acknowledge Him, and He shall direct thy paths.' Proverbs chapter three, verses five and six."

Jerry knew that sometime in the not too distant future he would need to remember those verses.

CHAPTER 12

The next day the two friends made their way up to the school to say a fond farewell to Mrs Turner and Miss Matherson, as well as the children and Michael. They had trusted that Michael would not breathe a word of their plans to anyone and on Monday morning it was clear that he had said nothing. Mrs Turner was bustling around as usual when Jerry and Linda entered. She stopped and looked at her two newest pupils.

"Oh, my dears," she said, placing a hand on each of their shoulders. "Such nice children to add to my school and only to stay here a couple of weeks. Ah well, it was a delight to get to know you both. I just wish you would stay until it is really safe for you to return. But you're leaving the island today and heading off to Portsmouth and from there, I suppose, to Jersey."

"Yes, something like that. We're not quite sure of all the details ourselves," Linda replied, smiling back at her and hoping to avoid any more questions. They had been told to tell people as little as possible.

Mrs Turner noticed her hesitancy. "It's all right, my dear," she said, speaking in a hushed tone. "I had a visit from Captain Cruickshank first thing this morning to explain why you were leaving and to tell me that I was not to tell anyone else. Your secret will be safe with me. I promise that."

"The navy has given us special permission," Linda whispered excitedly, pleased to have someone to confide in. "They will take us as close as they dare and then it's a case of us being paddled to Jersey by rubber dingy and climbing up the cliffs on the north coast. Then we'll go down to St. Helier and hopefully they will release Mum and Dad."

"I hope so too, but won't it be dangerous climbing those cliffs?"

"No, not really. They are about three hundred feet high but we'll find some way. Don't worry."

"Three hundred feet!" the head teacher replied in alarm. "You're having me on."

"No, she's not," Jerry said, "but hopefully we will land near a part that we can scramble up so we won't be climbing vertically up a rock face or anything like that."

"I'm glad about that," she replied as a tear came into her eye. She quickly wiped it away. "It's been lovely having you both at my school, if only for a short time. You will be missed most terribly. Take care of yourselves and when this awful war is over please come back and visit us here again."

"We will," the two friends promised. They walked down the corridor to look for Michael, and when they couldn't find him, called into their classroom to say farewell to Miss Matherson and the other children.

As they made to go out of the school to await Cuthbert, who had arranged to collect them in the jeep and take them back to the Griffiths', they heard a familiar voice calling to them. "Wait...er...wait a minute." They turned to see Michael running up the corridor towards them. "Just a minute. I... er...wanted to say thank you for what you have done for me whilst you were here."

"We were trying to find you," Jerry replied. "Where were you?"

"I was just a bit late; I thought I'd missed you."

"It's okay. We're still here," Linda reassured him.

"You two have made me realise what a horrible self-centred boy I was. I want to be different. I...er...want to be like you two."

"Michael," Jerry said, looking the older boy straight in the face, "we don't know much about the Bible, but we do know that it is God's Word and that it can change people's lives and destinies. It changed us forever when we came here and we believe that it can change you too."

"No, it's you two that have helped me to see how stupid I was."

"Not really. It was maybe God just using us. We prayed for you and we prayed on Saturday morning that we could do good to those who hated and hurt us. God answered that prayer as we were able to help rescue you from the river. You really need to thank God and not us for what has happened in your life."

Just then, a green army jeep swept into view and pulled up sharply on the road outside the school with a *toot toot* of the horn.

"Oh, Cuthbert's arrived early," Jerry said. "Listen, Michael. You get yourself a Bible and see if you can get yourself to the Sunday school at that thatched church down by Freshwater Bay."

The horn tooted again.

"Come on, Linda. I think we'd better go."

As they walked down the short path from the school entrance, they heard shouts and calls. They looked back to see that almost the whole school had gathered in the window fronting the road and were waving and calling to them. As they clambered into the jeep they could see Mrs Turner and Miss Matherson standing with Michael at the door.

Linda called back, "Thanks for everything. Take care. See you after the war!"

Jerry shouted to Michael over the noise of the children in the school. "Don't forget to get a Bible. Read it every day; it will help you to do the right thing."

They sat in the jeep, waving and smiling at the children who still called out to them through the open windows.

Cuthbert attempted to start the jeep but it just made a whirring noise. He tried again with the same result. "Oh, dear me," he said to himself. "The battery is still flat." Then turning to Jerry and Linda, he explained, "I'm sorry. I needed help starting this earlier because the battery was flat and I forgot about it when I turned the engine off. Will you help to give the jeep a push to get us started again?"

Without being asked, Mrs Turner turned to the children still hanging out of the windows and said, "Come on, children. The British Army requires our help!"

With that, a swarm of over thirty eager youngsters ran out of the school and began to push the jeep along the road. Cuthbert smiled at the sight of his vehicle being propelled by a whole school of children. When it was going quickly enough, he put it into second gear and lifted the clutch. The jeep shuddered, resisted and then suddenly burst into life and moved away from the crowd of children who stood in the road, laughing, waving and cheering until the jeep, along with Cuthbert, Jerry and Linda, disappeared around the corner and out of sight.

At the Griffiths' house, things were a little more subdued as Mrs Griffiths checked and rechecked that the two children had everything they required. "It's a long trip to Portsmouth," she said as she fussed and flapped around the children and the sergeant who stood watching with a smile on his face.

"Now, I've made you some Welsh cakes especially, because I know you like them and I've put in some bread made with the last of my flour ration for this week and a bit of homemade jam," Mrs Griffiths continued excitedly.

"How on earth do you expect Linda and Jerry to eat jam while they are travelling to Portsmouth?" her husband enquired disapprovingly.

"Well…" His wife thought for a while. "I thought it would keep till they got to Jersey. It's a sort of small present from their adoptive parents to their real ones."

"But they aren't brother and sister, you know," Cuthbert added, "so you'll need to give them a jar each. And," he added with a smile, "how will they ever carry a pot of jam from here to Jersey without breaking it?"

"Never mind that; these two will think of some way," Mrs Griffiths chided as she looked in the direction of the sergeant.

After a lot of hustle and bustle, things were ready, and the two children, with two small borrowed rucksacks, stood at the white front door of the Griffiths' house. Saying a last goodbye to the lady who had been like a mother to them for the past six weeks wasn't easy. Blodwyn Griffiths, usually busy, boisterous and full of life, was now very subdued. As she hugged both children she tried hard to keep the tears back. The thought of the two youngsters leaving her protective care and venturing once again onto the wild sea to go to an island home that had already been overrun by the might of the German army, made her feel very uneasy, but she knew they had to do it for Linda's parents' sake.

Eventually Cuthbert, who had remembered not to switch the engine off this time, drove the green army jeep away from the Griffiths' front door and along the road that led out of the village of Godshill that had been the children's home on the Isle of Wight. No one spoke as they watched Mr and Mrs Griffiths standing, waving and wiping tears from their eyes.

Jerry and Linda felt upset too, but they were also apprehensive about the outcome of the adventure ahead and whether they really would secure the release of Linda's parents.

"We travel up to Cowes to meet Brian," Cuthbert explained as he drove the jeep along the winding roads of the Isle of Wight. "From there, we all catch the ferry across to Southampton and from there, if good old Captain Cruickshank is to be believed, we will be taken by car straight down to Portsmouth."

Jerry, who was sat in the front, turned to look at Cuthbert. "I was looking on the map last night and Portsmouth is only just across there," he explained, waving his arm in some general direction. "Why couldn't we have just caught a ferry straight to Portsmouth without having to go to Southampton?"

"That's simple," Cuthbert explained. "There isn't a ferry that travels to Portsmouth from here. You have to go to Southampton."

"Oh," Jerry replied thoughtfully. "Wouldn't it be a good idea to start one?"

"Well, Jerry," the sergeant replied with a laugh, "maybe you could suggest it."

"I don't think anybody is going to take much notice of you, Jerry," Linda retorted with a grin.

"They have never required a ferry from here to Portsmouth in the past, so I can't think they will want one now."

"I suppose not, but it would have saved us a car journey from Southampton."

"Well, if you ask the driver of the ferry real nice-like, he might just divert to Portsmouth to drop you off there before he takes the other passengers to Southampton."

"Thanks," Jerry responded. "You never know. I might just do that!"

"Don't you dare! You will just embarrass us all," Linda exclaimed.

"Don't worry. I'm only joking."

Eventually the winding roads gave way to buildings as they entered East Cowes and headed towards the small ferry terminal. Here, the odd-looking vehicle ferry was waiting, and a small, deep-blue sports car was being driven up the loading ramps and on to the car deck. Another couple of vehicles were driven on before Cuthbert was waved forward in his army jeep. He pulled up just before the ramps in an area designated 'Military Vehicles Only', and all three jumped out.

"We have to go on foot," Cuthbert explained. "They require the jeep back at base. Anyway, it's better really, as we will have a big posh limousine provided by the Royal Navy to collect us from Southampton. Somebody else can sort out that flat battery!"

CHAPTER 13

After meeting up with Brian, the four made the short trip across the Solent towards Southampton. The sea was calm and the sky clear apart from a few wispy clouds that floated slowly across its blue expanse, changing shapes as they moved. Linda and Jerry enjoyed leaning over the metal railings, watching the sea froth up in tiny waves as the water broke away from the bows of the ferry.

"Have you ever heard of the *Titanic*?" Brian enquired as he joined the two children.

"Yes, of course we have," Jerry answered, turning to look at Brian. "She sank on her first journey after hitting an iceberg."

"Well, the *Titanic* had a sister ship just like it but ever so slightly smaller, called the *Olympic*. It had a serious accident here in the Solent a year before *Titanic* sank."

"Wow! I never knew that. What happened?"

"*Olympic* and a Royal Navy ship called HMS *Hawke* were cruising along side by side when somehow *Olympic* turned across the path of *Hawke* and the two collided. The bow of *Hawke* was badly mangled and the ship very nearly capsized. There were two big holes torn in the side of *Olympic*, but I don't think anyone was killed. The captain of *Olympic* was the captain of *Titanic* when it sank," Brian concluded.

"All I can say," Linda added, standing upright from her leaning position on the rail, "is that I hope the Royal Navy don't bump into anything when we are sailing with them."

The ferry eventually arrived at Southampton and came to a stop with a small bump. It lowered its ramp down onto a concrete slipway in order to allow the few vehicles on board to drive off.

"Papers, please," a man in uniform demanded from the passengers as they began to disembark down the short gangway that had been lowered from the boat to the shore. Cuthbert handed over the papers to the uniformed man, who took them and glanced over them. "I've a message for you in the office. Just wait here while I check the other passengers."

The two children and two soldiers moved to one side to allow the rest of the passengers to walk down the gangway and off the ferry. Once all the people had been checked off, the man signalled to the four to follow him along the concrete ramp to a small building built with brick and wood. Once inside, he pulled a piece of paper from off a very untidy desk. "Telegram," he announced austerely, "from Royal Navy logistics, Portsmouth. Please inform army staff escorting two children. Transport delayed. Vehicular pickup to take place later this evening. Tell sergeant in charge to ring Portsmouth 9567 upon arrival."

"Oh, no!" Brian said as he let out a deep breath. "We should have brought the jeep."

"Can I borrow your phone, please?" Cuthbert asked the official.

"Yes, you may," the man replied, losing his air of authority. "Just don't be too long as it's we who pay the bill, not the army."

After a short conversation, Cuthbert replaced the receiver. "It looks like we have a few hours to kill here in Southampton," he explained. "Trust the navy to leave the army high and dry just when we need them. The staff car is on official business and won't be available until later, and apparently no other vehicles are available to collect us. So what do you young folks want to do for the next four hours?"

"Um," Jerry responded in a rather unenthusiastic manner. He was really rather anxious to get on with the next part of their journey. "My father always says something like 'always try to make time count by reading or discovering something that will educate you', so I guess we could visit any sights that could be of interest, if there is nothing better to do."

"Okay, see the town it is," Cuthbert replied. "And if we see anyone who we think maybe could help us, we will ask them...for instance, that policeman across the street," he added, looking out the window of the small building they were in. Without waiting for a response from the others, Cuthbert started to jog across the road, dodging a cyclist and waiting in the middle of the road for a small black car to pass by before finally catching up with the police constable.

Linda and Jerry found it hard to keep straight faces as they watched Cuthbert and the policeman engage in an animated conversation with raising of arms and the waving of hands in various directions as the policeman tried to point Cuthbert in the direction of things which would 'educate' the two children.

After a few minutes of what appeared to be a game of verbal tennis, Cuthbert came back smiling broadly.

"Well, you can always count on the bobby on the beat to be helpful just when you need him. The bombing of the city last year, especially at the end of November, has left High Street in ruins, but he says we can walk over there and find Berth 44," he said, waving an arm expressively in the direction of the sea.

"And what is Berth 44?" Brian asked with a disapproving look.

"Berth 44? Berth 44?" Cuthbert retorted in mock surprise. "You don't know what Berth 44 is famous for?"

"No, I don't," Brian answered honestly. "And neither did you until you spoke to that bobby, I bet."

"Well...actually, no, I didn't," the sergeant confessed. "Berth 44 is where the great passenger ship *Titanic* was berthed over Easter 1912 before it set sail, never to return."

"She," Jerry butted in.

"Pardon?" Cuthbert asked.

"She," the boy again repeated. "You called the *Titanic* 'it' but every ship is a lady so you should have called it 'she'!"

"Yes, quite right," Brian joined in with a mischievous twinkle in his eye. "Fancy my sergeant not knowing that all ships are 'she's'."

Cuthbert ignored the fun that was being made of him and commenced walking along the pathway on the side of the road.

After a short but brisk walk, they arrived at a dock and Cuthbert spoke to an important-looking man walking towards them.

"Yes, Berth 44," the stranger repeated as he sucked in his breath and considered the question as if pondering some great mathematical problem. "Well now, if you walk on down here and come to the sea, you'll see a concrete jetty sticking out into the water. Walk three-quarters of the way down and look at the bollard placed on the seaward side. That's the very same bollard *Titanic* was moored to before she sailed. You will have walked right along the length of Berth 44, just as the passengers on that great ship did twenty-nine years ago."

"Wow," Cuthbert replied, clearly impressed, as he thanked the man and continued to lead the way. "Just think, folks, we will be standing on a little piece of history."

"Don't you think," Linda spoke after being quiet for some time, "that this war against Hitler, Germany and the Nazis is history?"

"Well, yes, I guess it will be…"

Cuthbert's voice was suddenly drowned out by the wailing of an air raid siren in the distance. Someone hurried past, shouting, "Don't just stand there! Get to the shelter!"

Suddenly, instinct took over as all four broke into a mad run, following the man who obviously knew where he was going. As they passed an old red brick building, they could see someone else making for what appeared to be a very crude and basic shelter in a small area of grassland. It had a corrugated metal roof covered with what looked like earth and rubble. They dashed down three steps and entered through the open door. Once it was full of those wishing to shelter from what all thought was another imminent air raid, the person closest to the wooden door shut it and flipped the latch to keep it closed.

"Have you ever been in one of these before?" Brian asked as he shuffled on the hard wooden benches, trying to make himself comfortable.

"No, we haven't," Jerry answered, looking around at the poorly constructed and rather damp interior.

"This is an Anderson shelter. It's just made out of wood, corrugated metal and earth, plus whatever other materials were available at the time. It's cheap, but pretty effective at keeping those inside safe."

"So would it keep us safe if a bomb landed directly on top of us?" Linda asked, looking up at the roof.

"No, it certainly wouldn't," Cuthbert interjected. "However, it should protect us from the blast and splinters if one landed nearby."

"Another air raid!" a woman sitting further along the bench grumbled to no one in particular. "You'd have thought they'd give us a break. After all, they have just about destroyed the city centre, and there's not much left of High Street."

"You rightly know, Ethel, it's not the city they are out to destroy. It's the docklands. They bomb anywhere that our warships might berth," a smart-looking elderly gentleman sitting opposite her replied, before adding, "It's a complete waste of their time doing this, though. No matter how many bombs fall, we will never give in!"

After a further fifteen minutes or so, the sound of the all clear siren wailed outside the small and increasingly uncomfortable shelter. The man sitting closest to the old wooden door lifted the latch and gave it a shove to open it. Everyone breathed a sigh of relief as the light flooded the dark interior and fresh air replaced the stale, musty atmosphere.

"Another false alarm," someone said as they climbed out into the open.

"Phew," Jerry sighed, taking a deep breath. "That was nearly as dramatic as when we were bombed in Jersey last year, even if nothing did happen."

"Well, it was very frightening to me," said Linda.

"I don't suppose you've heard too many German Heinkels and Dorniers coming over?" Cuthbert enquired.

"Well, I think I'd rather not if they are dropping bombs. It was frightening enough in Jersey. I don't really want to see another German air raid, especially where people get killed like they did in Jersey," Jerry replied with a frown.

"Come on, then," urged Brian. "Let's have a look at where *Titanic* was berthed and then what's left of Southampton city centre, shall we?"

CHAPTER 14

"Berth 44, my lady," Brian teased looking at Linda as the four walked down a long jetty in the docks area. "So this is where the great *Titanic* was berthed over Easter 1912 before she set off on her tragic journey into history."

"Can't you just imagine all those people walking along here and going up the gangways into that wonderful ship?" Jerry exclaimed.

"I suppose so," Cuthbert mumbled without much enthusiasm. "I just find it hard to visualise. To me, this is just a berth from which many ships have left, not just one that sank on its first trip."

"Oh, Cuthbert," Brian retorted with a laugh. "You can be so totally boring at times. I can imagine you and I at some time fighting in Germany and old Adolf Hitler comes over to us with his hands up to surrender and you just say, 'Come along, Adolf, to see my commanding officer. You are under arrest.' Everything is just so matter of fact with you, Sergeant!"

"What would you say?" enquired Linda, eagerly looking at Brian.

"What do you mean?" Brian answered, a look of confusion spreading across his face.

"What would you say if Adolf Hitler surrendered to you?"

"Oh, I see," he chuckled. "I wouldn't say anything to him at all. I'd just shoot him."

The four of them fell about laughing at Brian's answer.

"Oy! You lot! What's going on here?" A soldier, in peaked cap with a red band, came striding along the berth towards them.

"Oh, dear," Cuthbert groaned. "A military policeman."

"So what's the big idea?" the man questioned as he drew

nearer. "What are you doing here and how did you gain access to the docks?"

After several minutes of explanation from Cuthbert and Brian, along with the showing of their identity papers, the four were allowed by the military policeman to leave the docks area and head into the city.

"Really, this officialdom," Cuthbert moaned as they walked away from Berth 44. "That policeman could see we were in uniform and would have known that we had already shown our papers to obtain access, but still he has to come along, throwing his weight around and showing off his red-banded peaked cap as if he's more important than anyone else."

"Well, at least he didn't shoot us like Brian said he'd do to Hitler if he saw him," Jerry replied, smiling mischievously.

"No, no. It could have been worse," the sergeant answered, smiling back. "But then, I have never as yet been mistaken for Adolf Hitler!"

"What does the red band on his hat signify?" Linda asked inquisitively.

"It's to show that he is a military policeman," Brian replied.

"Yes, and some of them think because they wear it they own the place," Cuthbert retorted. "I think somehow we slipped past a barrier in the confusion of the air raid warning. That's why he was a bit annoyed. Come on, let's get going into the city."

"Hey, take a look at this," Linda called excitedly. "It's a memorial about the *Stella*."

"Who was Stella?" asked Brian with interest.

"*Stella* was the channel ferry that sank after running into the Casquets rocks at the end of the 1800s. My parents told me all about it," Linda replied.

"I heard about that at school," Jerry exclaimed. "The captain had a strange name. I think he was called Captain Reeks. How funny!"

"Listen to this," Linda continued, as she read the dedication on a plaque inside the strange six-pillared, stone-roofed memorial. " 'In memory of the heroic death of Mary Anne Rogers, stewardess of the *Stella* who, on the night of the thirtieth of March, 1899, amid the confusion and terror of shipwreck, aided all the women under her charge to quit the vessel in safety.' "

"So she saved all the women on board," Brian interrupted.

"I haven't finished yet," Linda scolded. "There's more. Listen. 'Giving her own lifebelt to one who was unprotected, urged by the sailors to make sure her escape, she refused, lest she might endanger the heavily-laden boat. Cheering the departing crew with the friendly cry of 'Good-bye, good-bye,' she was seen a few moments later as the *Stella* went down, lifting her arms upwards with the prayer, 'Lord, have me,' then sank in the waters with the sinking ship.

"Actions such as these, revealing steadfast performance of duty in the face of death, ready self-sacrifice for the sake of others, reliance on God, constitute the glorious heritage of our English race. They deserve perpetual commemoration, because among the trivial pleasures and sordid strife of the world, they recall to us forever the nobility and love-worthiness of human nature.' "

"Wow! So that lady died after rescuing all those others," Jerry said, puffing out his cheeks as he considered her gallant sacrifice.

"Yes, she did," Linda said thoughtfully as she re-read the words on the memorial. "I wonder if they made a mistake."

"Of course they made a mistake running into the Casker... Caser...those rocks you mentioned," Cuthbert exclaimed.

"Casquets," Jerry added helpfully. "They are a group of rocks and a very dangerous reef about six miles west of Alderney. The *Stella* wasn't the first ship to sink there either and she probably won't be the last."

"I don't know how the army got mixed up with you two," Brian laughed. "You'd both be much better off with the navy!"

"I wasn't talking about the mistake of the ship sinking, but what was written about the last words of that stewardess,"

Linda said. "It says that she said, 'Lord, have me,' but I think she might have said, 'Lord, save me.' "

"Why?" asked Brian interestedly.

"Because I read the words 'Lord, save me' in Uncle Fred's Bible the other day and underlined them because they were so good. If I remember, they were spoken by one of the disciples, I think it was Peter, when he was sinking in the sea. He said, 'Lord, save me.' I think that would have made more sense for her to have said than 'Lord, have me.' Don't you?

"Oh, absolutely. I totally agree with you," Cuthbert replied with a mischievous smile. "Never mind the navy, Brian, I think she'd make a good archbishop!"

"But what if she was a Christian and ready to go to heaven?" Jerry said thoughtfully as he moved closer to read the inscription himself. "I mean, that would make perfect sense if she knew she was going to die and was ready for heaven. It seems to me that she was almost reaching out her arms, asking the Lord to take her to heaven."

"I hadn't thought of that," Linda replied. "I think you're right."

"But thinking about it again," Cuthbert added, "the Lord wouldn't save her just like that a few seconds before she died. No way, He'd expect her to live a bit and prove her sincerity before saving her. Yes, Jerry's definitely right on this one, Linda."

"But, Cuthbert," said Jerry, "I read a little while ago in the Bible of the robber who died on the cross next to the Lord Jesus. When he asked the Lord to save him, He did, and he was just about to die too. I can't remember the exact words, but Jesus told him he was going to heaven. So someone can become a Christian just before they die, but it's a bit dangerous."

"Why is it dangerous?" asked Brian as he leaned against one of the stone pillars, trying to read the inscription himself.

"Well, what if you wait until you die and then you die so suddenly that you don't have time to trust the Lord?" Jerry answered.

"Um, I hadn't thought of that," Brian said thoughtfully as he carefully read the story of Mary Anne Rogers once again.

"So this is a case for that brilliant detective, Sherlock Holmes," Cuthbert interjected, "to find out if Mary Rogers' final words were 'Lord, save me,' or as it's recorded here, 'Lord, have me'? I wonder what conclusion the great detective would make, apart from the obvious fact that there is just one letter difference?"

"That's easy," Linda again responded, moving away from the pillar and inscription. "Firstly, Sherlock Holmes would interview Mary Rogers' family and friends."

"Why?" asked Brian, standing up straight and stretching out his back, having read the story of the stewardess' final acts.

"Because her family would know if Mary Rogers really was a Christian before the *Stella* sank. That is, if any of them are still alive today."

"And how would they know that?" Cuthbert enquired, looking earnestly at both youngsters.

"Well, maybe by what she had told them, or maybe by how she lived her life."

"Oh, you mean if she went to church?"

"Not necessarily," Jerry retorted. "Anyone can go to church and not be a Christian. No, I think there would be other things that would be obvious in her life like..." He bent down and rummaged through the little bag he was carrying before pulling out Uncle Fred's worn and well-read little black Bible. "Like having a Bible like this that is read every day, or did she pray, or was she kind or..."

"All right, all right, I think I get your point," Cuthbert answered with a chuckle. "Sherlock Holmes would put all these things together and then if she showed these characteristics, he would think that she was praying, 'Lord, have me,' because she already was a Christian, but if she did not show any of the things you just mentioned it would probably mean she wasn't a Christian and in her dying breath was praying, 'Lord, save me.' "

"You've got it!" Linda answered, with a smile that almost met her ears.

"Um," Brian pondered seriously. "My Sunday school teacher used to say that salvation not only changed a person's destiny by making them fit for heaven but also their life by changing their behaviour."

"Well, I don't know much about the Bible yet," Jerry replied, looking down at the ground, "but I do know that when my Uncle Fred trusted the Lord Jesus in Belfast, it changed his life from a wild drunkard to a sensible, kind, caring person. I also know that since I have trusted the Lord, I have wanted to think more about good things and haven't wanted to use bad or unkind words."

"Me too," added Linda excitedly. "The more I read the Bible and the more I pray, although I find praying really hard, the less I want to do anything that God would not be happy about me doing. Trusting the Lord Jesus really does totally change your life and how you think. Don't you want to become Christians and have your lives changed too?"

"Well, er, I sort of, um, er…That's a good question," Brian stuttered.

Peep peep! A large navy-blue car pulled up on the road next to them and a tall young man in a Royal Navy uniform climbed out from the driver's seat. "Excuse me," he said with a shy smile, addressing Cuthbert. "You wouldn't happen to be Sergeant Rennoldson, would you?"

"Yes, I am," Cuthbert replied in surprise.

"Ah. I'm Petty Officer Barnswick. I have been detailed to collect two soldiers and two children from Southampton and drive them to our submarine base in Portsmouth."

"Oh, good!" Brian enthused, smiling. "I was beginning to think that we had been left high and dry by the navy."

"I'm very sorry," the petty officer responded as he moved round to open the rear doors of the large and rather expensive-looking vehicle. "We had a flap on this morning with the unexpected visit of an admiral and I had to drive him to Chichester and then double back to pick you up. I'm very sorry if you have been waiting a long time."

"No, no. It's been a most interesting wait. We have been doing some detective work on the last words of a lady who died on a ship forty-two years ago," Cuthbert answered vaguely to the bemused naval rating as he followed Linda and Jerry into the car. "It's been most entertaining," he concluded with a smile and wink at the two children.

CHAPTER 15

"Wow!" Jerry exclaimed as he climbed into the car and looked at the two rows of seats facing each other in the interior. "Can I sit here?" he asked, pointing to the bench seat that faced towards the rear. "I've never been in a car like this before."

"Before coming over here I had hardly ever been in a car at all," Linda added awkwardly. "In Jersey, if we want to go anywhere we hitch up the horse to the cart or just walk."

"Well, I reckon that once this war's over, motorcars will be more popular than ever," Brian commented as he closed the door and took his seat next to Cuthbert, facing the two children.

"This is the staff car," Petty Officer Barnswick said as he set off with a start. "It's designed to allow face-to-face conversation between officers travelling in the back."

Jerry and Linda kept looking out through the rear window as the car sped along the roads and lanes between Southampton and Portsmouth. Eventually they left the countryside and came into another heavily built-up area where the evidence of bomb damage could be seen in the form of burnt-out and derelict houses and factories. There was also the occasional pile of rubble that had obviously been a building at some stage.

The car skirted the city before slowing as it approached a barrier manned by two men in uniform who were wearing red-topped peaked hats.

"Redcaps," Brian whispered. "Military policemen again."

"Your papers, please," one of the two official-looking men asked as he peered into the car through the window that Cuthbert had opened.

Brian and Cuthbert handed over the relevant papers and passes which were carefully scrutinised by the policemen.

"And who are these two?" one of them enquired as he bent down and motioned in the direction of Jerry and Linda through the opened window.

"Oh, we are escorting them to join the Third Flotilla Submarine Corps here at HMNB Portsmouth," Cuthbert answered, smiling.

"Whatever does HMNB stand for?" asked Linda.

"His Majesty's Naval Base," the policeman answered, smiling at both children.

"So you're going to be our two new submariner recruits, are you?" he continued pleasantly, before adding, "All in order," and handing back the papers to the two soldiers. He saluted smartly and waved the car through whilst his colleague raised the barrier.

The car drove rapidly past various offices and stores as well as around some holes which were clearly bomb craters, before coming to a halt outside a red brick building with dark-blue painted window frames. Here, Petty Officer Barnswick stepped out and opened the car doors to allow his occupants to clamber out of their seats. He then led them through a set of double doors and into a large room with various maps and charts covering the walls.

"Aha! Well, hello!" a friendly-looking man said as he turned around from the table, where he was busily writing, to face the group. "I am Captain Lewis and I believe that I have been given the pleasure of looking after your travel arrangements to Jersey by way of one of our submarines."

He stood up and walked towards the four who were standing with the petty officer. Jerry observed the crisp smartness of his dark-blue Royal Navy uniform. Linda noticed that he was tall but with soft brown eyes, which seemed to shine with warmth as he approached, hand outstretched ready to shake theirs.

"I've heard all about your story," he enthused as he vigorously shook the hands of the two youngsters, "how you escaped from Jersey right under the noses of the German army and then lost your uncle in Guernsey before sailing right up the Channel and being shipwrecked on the Isle of Wight." His speech was fast but clear as he commended the two for their bravery. "We could do with more plucky youngsters like you two. There will be many sacrifices made before this war comes to an end. Anyway, you are now here because we have orders from the highest level to get you both back to Jersey to secure the release of some important prisoners. It's been decided that the safest way to accomplish this tricky task is to take you as close to the Island as we can by submarine."

"It sounds exciting," Jerry exclaimed. "I really can't believe that we are actually going to travel in a submarine."

"Well, it's not the way I'd choose to travel but if it will get us to Jersey, I'm all for it," Linda interjected. "I've never been that happy to have my face in the water, never mind to go completely underwater. I hope I get on okay in a metal box hundreds of feet below the sea."

"Oh, you'll be all right, young miss, er, Linda, isn't it? Today's submarines are vastly superior to those in the last war and you'll never be much more than a hundred to a hundred and fifty feet below the surface. The English Channel is not too deep, except about thirty or so miles north of Guernsey where it drops to around six hundred feet."

"But we'll have to go past Guernsey to Jersey. Will we have to go hundreds of feet deep there?" Linda asked.

"No, no!" Captain Lewis patiently explained. "Our submarines do not hug the seafloor; that's much too dangerous. They prefer to stay hidden just under the surface so they can use their periscopes to see what's happening on the surface."

Upon hearing this Linda felt a little more confident.

"Oh, Linda, we'll be just fine," Jerry responded with enthusiasm.

"Excuse me," Cuthbert broke in, "but none of us have eaten since we left the Isle of Wight this morning. Is there a mess room where we could go and get something?"

"Oh, yes, of course, of course. How very remiss of me," the

captain said, clearly embarrassed at his oversight. "Just follow me and we'll get you all fed before we explain the training you'll be undertaking in the next few days."

Over a hearty meal of stew, mashed potato and carrots, the two soldiers and the Royal Navy captain discussed with Jerry and Linda the adventure they were about to undertake.

"You'll travel to Scotland tomorrow," the captain explained, "where you will join our newly formed Twelfth Submarine Flotilla, which is a highly specialised unit being put together in order to launch attacks against enemy positions that our conventional weapons will not reach. You will then stay a night at our headquarters on the Isle of Bute on the River Clyde, downstream from Glasgow, before you go north to Kylesku to undergo basic training for two days."

"So are we not travelling to Jersey from Portsmouth?" Linda asked, slightly troubled at the rather complicated arrangements that seemed to have been made.

"No. You will probably go from Holy Loch on the Clyde River. It's much too dangerous to operate submarines out of Portsmouth on a regular basis," the captain explained. "We are sending you all to Scotland for training because it has the best and newest equipment to prepare you for submarine travel. I know it's a long way and a good day's journey on the train, but the benefits will be great for you all."

"Just a minute," Brian interjected. "You keep saying about us 'all'. I thought we were handing responsibility for Jerry and Linda over to the Royal Navy from now on."

"Yes, that would usually be the case. However, it has been requested by those in higher ranks that you continue to chaperone Jerry and Linda until they are safely returned to Jersey."

"So are we to travel in this submarine too?" Brian asked in surprise.

Jerry looked at him with amusement. He could see that Brian wasn't too keen on the idea. "Don't you like the thought of travelling on a submarine?" he questioned. "It's just a sort of exciting adventure, but underwater, that's all."

"Hum! Well, I don't like flying, that's why I didn't join the Royal Air Force, and I'm not too keen on water, that's why I never joined the navy. I'd really prefer to stay on land. It seems to be much safer," Brian answered flatly. "Well, if I have to go across the English Channel in a submarine, then I have to go. Where did you say we sail from once our training is over?"

"Holy Loch on the River Clyde. You'll sail down the west coast and out into the Channel. It will take you a good day and a half to complete the journey," Captain Lewis confidently affirmed, "but it should have Jerry and Linda in Jersey by the seventeenth. That gives us three days to spare. It's the twentieth you have to be back by, isn't it?"

"Well," said Cuthbert, raising his eyebrows in recognition of the facts that had just been placed before him. "I guess its 'goodbye' to the south coast of England and 'hello' to bonny Scotland!"

"Why do they always call Scotland 'bonny'?" Linda asked eagerly.

"If I was you I'd wait until you get there, young lady," the captain answered as he placed his knife and fork onto his empty plate and moved it away. "If you have any appreciation of natural beauty, you will soon see why our beloved northern neighbour is called bonny. It is, in my opinion, the most beautiful part of the British Isles."

"Is it more beautiful than Jersey?" Linda enquired eagerly.

"That I am unable to say because I have never been to Jersey. I tell you what, though," the captain replied, "you let me know what you think of it compared with Jersey when you get there."

"You're on," Linda said excitedly, smiling at the officer. "I'll give you a full report. Scotland, here we come!"

"Oh no," grumbled Cuthbert in fun. "Not only is she going to be an archbishop and join the navy, but she will probably start selling holidays to Scotland or Jersey or maybe even both!"

CHAPTER 16

The four travellers stretched and yawned as they stepped out of the overnight sleeper train that had brought them up the west coast of England and into the centre of Glasgow. Wearily, they made their way along the concourse of the station, Jerry and Linda turning up their noses at the smell of burning coal and steam produced by the engine that had pulled their train all the way from London.

"Well, that was an amazingly long train journey," Jerry exclaimed as he looked around the station with wide-eyed wonder.

"I've never seen a train with beds in it either," Linda enthused as she too looked all around the station and at the various naval personnel also exiting the train.

"Hey," Jerry called out, "why were so many men from the navy on board our train?"

"Some are probably coming back after leave to join their ships on the River Clyde, or maybe they are going across to Edinburgh to join other ships in Rosyth," Cuthbert answered.

"But, then again, some might be intending to fly up to the Orkney Islands in order to join other fleet ships in Scapa Flow," chipped in Brian, feeling glad he had done his homework on the activities of the navy before he left Portsmouth.

"What is Scapa Flow?" Linda asked, looking at Brian.

"That's the main anchorage for the Home Fleet. It was used in the last war, sort of as the headquarters of the Royal Navy and they are using it again during this war."

"It's a large natural harbour that allows some protection to Royal Navy ships." Cuthbert was also eager to show off his somewhat limited knowledge of the activities of the navy. "It's a long way from German airfields, so that makes it relatively safe from air attack, although a German U-boat did manage to get into it just a month after the war started and sank *Royal Oak*, one of our biggest ships."

"That was a real sad affair," Brian added. "I remember it happening. Hundreds of sailors, one minute asleep in their bunks and the next drowning in the freezing water."

"I hope we don't die in this submarine," stated Linda, still having misgivings about their journey.

"No, no. Not at all. Safe as houses are British submarines," Cuthbert answered, trying to be positive for Linda's sake. "I can't think of anything that can really go wrong. They wouldn't be letting us go if they thought there was any real danger."

"And hopefully most of it will be on the surface, not underwater," another deep voice chipped in from behind the group, making them all swing round in surprise. "Good morning. I'm Commodore Harewood from the Twelfth Submarine Flotilla. I am presuming that I have the pleasure of addressing...er...let me see now," he fumbled in his pocket, obviously looking for a piece of paper. "Ah! Here it is. A telegram sent from Captain Lewis in Portsmouth. You must be Sergeant Rennoldson, Corporal Brian Oliver, Jerry Le Godel and Linda De La Haye?"

"Correct on every count," Brian answered with a twinkle in his eye.

"Well, I must say my commanding officer is playing absolute billy-o about you all being thrust on us at Bute and Kylesku, he really is. Says it's a massive waste of money and manpower, just to return two children to Jersey. He says that they should never have left in the first place." He smiled as he looked at both Jerry and Linda. "But I say it'll be nice having someone other than foul-mouthed seamen and able seamen around the place for a few days."

"I'm not sure your commanding officer has all the information about this escapade, but maybe that's as well. You won't have any trouble with these two, I can tell you," Brian replied. "They're as good as gold."

"And twice as valuable," Cuthbert chipped in with unusual warmth.

"It's these two you need to look out for," Jerry countered, not missing an opportunity to have a bit of fun with the two soldiers who had been so kind to them since their arrival on the Isle of Wight.

Commodore Harewood smiled, and looking the two soldiers up and down, replied, "Yes, I can see that. The Royal Navy has often been called upon to sort out the mess left by the army."

"Whatever do you mean…mess left by the army?" Brian asked, straightening himself so as to tower over the smaller Royal Navy man.

"Gallipoli in the last war; Dunkirk last year," the commodore answered, smiling. "It was the navy on both occasions who had to do the lion's share of rescuing the army."

"Um, well, the army was put in a hopeless situation in both those places. It wasn't our fault."

"No, I guess not. The army never makes any mistakes, do they?" the navy officer responded light-heartedly. "Anyway, we are very happy to help you land lovers out once again in trying to get these two young…Whatever is going on there?"

As they walked out of the station, their attention was drawn by the shrill sound of a policeman's whistle and then to a young man racing through the crowds of people on the opposite side of the road. A few yards behind him, the policeman was running hard in pursuit while blowing frantically on his whistle to gain help from other policemen in the area.

"Hey, it's a police chase!" Jerry blurted out with excitement as he watched the young man open a wooden door and disappear into one of the tenements across from the railway station. "Let's go and see what's going on," he enthused as he made to cross the road.

"No, wait!" called Cuthbert as Jerry crossed the road in time to see the policeman knocking frantically on the door.

Just then, the door released a little, and the policeman pushed it hard until it was nearly fully open. However, as he stepped to go in, the door suddenly slammed back against him with such force that it sent him reeling back out of the doorway and down a couple of steps. He landed sprawling in the street, blood flowing freely from his nose. At the same time, the young man he had been chasing darted out from behind the door and bounded out of the entrance, right past where Jerry was now standing. Without stopping to think, Jerry instinctively put his leg out, tripping the young man and causing him to join the policeman sprawling on the road. As he tried to pick himself up, Cuthbert, Brian and Commodore Harewood leapt on him, pinning him to the ground.

"Get off of me," the man cried as he struggled in vain to break the hold the three men had on him. "Let me go, ye ken," he called again, still struggling.

As they held him, another policeman arrived and took over from Brian, who went to assist the injured policeman who was sitting where he had fallen, dazed and bleeding.

Within a few minutes, two more policemen arrived, and taking the young man roughly, they handcuffed him and marched him into the railway station to call for transport to take him to the police station.

"What did he do?" Jerry asked the injured policeman who was now standing next to Brian, holding a handkerchief to his nose.

"Snatched a purse from an old wifey down the road."

"Old wifey?" Brian enquired, fixing the policeman with an interested stare.

"He means an old lady," the naval officer helpfully interjected. "It's a sort of Scottish dialect."

"Oh, I see," Brian responded, still looking puzzled.

"I wanna thank ye, son," the policeman said, turning to Jerry, still holding his rapidly-reddening handkerchief to his nose. "That were quick thinking of you, ye ken, to trip him like that. Stopped him from getting clean away."

" 'Ye ken' means 'you know', before you ask," the commander explained.

"Oh, I see! It's a strange language they speak up here." Brian smiled back.

"It was a fair old fall you gave him," Linda added, joining the conversation. "Did you see how he went flying after hitting your leg, Jerry?"

"Yes, I saw," Jerry answered, looking at the place where the young man had fallen. "I never really thought about it. I just knew I should do something to help stop him but I didn't really think it would work."

"These two don't half get themselves in some fixes." Cuthbert turned to his naval companion. "Since being washed up on the Isle of Wight, they have been to see some of the most important men in London, rescued people from drowning on a river and now they catch a criminal. Something tells me we are in for more adventures before we say goodbye to these two youngsters."

A little later they found themselves at the local police station, making a statement about what had happened.

"Thank you so much for your help," said the police inspector in his dark-blue uniform with two pips on each shoulder, as he shook Jerry vigorously by his hand. "That young hoodlum has been running amok round the streets of Glasgow for some time so I'm glad we have him now safely under lock and key."

"Well, I didn't really do much," Jerry answered, rather embarrassed by the praise he was receiving. He looked up at the tall, lean inspector who had been addressing him. "I just happened to be in the right place at the right time. It's what anyone else would have done if they'd seen what I saw."

"That may be so," the inspector replied, "but not everyone wants to get involved these days and give the police force the help it sometimes needs." He opened the door to let the five of them out. "Thank you again," he echoed as they made their way along the path away from the police station.

"You know," Brian whispered in a conspiratorial way to Cuthbert, "I think you're right. Adventure does seem to follow these two young ones wherever they go. I just hope that it doesn't come calling in any large doses when we are in that submarine underneath the English Channel!"

CHAPTER 17

"Welcome to the Twelfth Submarine Flotilla," Lieutenant Commodore Harewood said as the five clambered out of a small motorboat that had carried them across the River Clyde to the Isle of Bute. "This is Port Bannatyne where we are based. You will be staying in HMS Varbel."

"Oh, great," Jerry exclaimed enthusiastically. "We will be staying on board a ship."

"No, no!" The commodore laughed. "HMS Varbel is a hotel that we have taken over. Most places used by the navy are given HMS titles."

"Oh," Jerry responded, with a look of disappointment.

"Well, I'm certainly pleased not to be staying on a ship," Cuthbert announced. "Never did really take to sailing."

"Hey, what's that tower?" Linda enquired, looking up at a very tall, square grey tower just outside the town.

"Oh, that's our SETT," Commodore Harewood replied. "You'll all be having a go in that after lunch."

"And just what is your SETT?" Brian asked.

"Sorry. That's our Submarine Escape Training Tank. It is one hundred feet high and allows you to learn how to escape from a submarine."

"How does it work?" asked Cuthbert suspiciously, looking across at the structure and scratching his head.

"It's filled with water and we flood a capsule that you will be sitting in. You have to open an escape hatch and swim to the top of the tower."

"Underwater?" Cuthbert asked hesitatingly.

"Well, yes, of course," the commodore replied with a smile. "If you are going to escape from a submarine I guess it's likely to be underwater and not flying through the air!"

"Umm," Brian breathed in, pursing his lips. "Er, how high did you say that tower was?"

"Only one hundred feet," Commodore Harewood said, his smile increasing to a broad grin. "It's really nothing at all to worry about; I have done it many times."

"I must say," Jerry butted in, "it sounds quite exciting having to swim right up to the top of that tower."

"I'm not sure," Linda added nervously.

"Me neither," Cuthbert moaned. "I'll never be able to hold my breath that long."

Commodore Harewood burst into fits of laughter. "Oh, really, you won't have to hold your breath. You have a little oxygen tank with about a thirty-minute air supply that you wear. It only takes a few seconds to rise one hundred feet as long as you remember to breath out once you have got out of your capsule. You also have a pair of goggles so that you can see. It's a doddle, really it is."

"Oh, well, if we have oxygen and goggles, I might be okay," Linda responded, relaxing a little. "I wonder what your Uncle Fred would make of all this after all his years at sea?"

A shadow fell across Jerry's face as he looked across at his friend. "You know, Linda, in all the events that have happened in this past week or so, I haven't thought much about Uncle Fred. I suppose he'll go to prisoner of war camp. We really must pray for him more. I do hope he is all right."

"Who is Uncle Fred?" the commodore enquired.

"He's my uncle who got captured by the Germans when we were in Guernsey. That's why we had to come up the Channel to England on our own. He's now a prisoner in Guernsey. He told Linda and me about his faith in God. That helped us on our journey across the English Channel. Now we try to read his Bible every day."

"He was obviously a brave man."

"'Yes, he was. He told us how one night he became a Christian in Belfast and then he missed his ship out of port. He had to get another one and when he reached Southampton he found that his ship had been sunk by a German U-boat."

"It's bizarre, really. Here we are, about to go on a submarine to return home, and Uncle Fred missed being killed by a submarine in the last war," Linda remarked.

Two hours later, Jerry and a rather nervous-looking Linda, plus two apprehensive soldiers, were preparing to be locked into a capsule that was built to represent a submarine stuck underwater. Along with them was an experienced sailor from the submarine flotilla.

"This is Able Seaman Scott McGregor. He's one of the most experienced submariners we have and an expert at submarine escape techniques," Commodore Harewood explained as he introduced the group to the sailor who was kitted out like them with a small rubber oxygen pack and life vest attached to his chest.

"Wow," he said as he looked at the two children and smiled in surprise. "It's the first time we have had such young recruits training for submarine duties."

"Er, um," Jerry stammered, "not exactly. We are going to catch a submarine so we can travel home to Jersey."

"Strike a light!" Scott replied in disbelief. "Don't tell me that the Royal Navy is now running a ferry service by submarine to Jersey!"

"Not quite," Commodore Harewood interrupted. "It's a long story, Scott. I'll fill you in later. For now, all you need to know is that our orders come from the very highest level, so we have to ensure that these two youngsters and these two members of our noble army know how to escape from a submarine in the event of an emergency."

"Right, sir. Leave them to me, sir," the submariner added as he started to close the watertight door between him and the commodore.

"Oh, just one more thing," Commodore Harewood added as he stopped the door swinging closed. "Please don't drown these army chaps, otherwise there will be a right rumpus down at the Admiralty."

"Right, sir. I'll try my best to keep them safe, sir. Don't want the senior service to be the death of these here land lovers, do we?" He smiled at Cuthbert and Brian as he pulled the door closed with a slam and pushed down hard on the long lever to secure it.

"Okay, remember that when I start flooding this place, do not move, and don't start to undo that escape door up there until this is full and we are all underwater. Put these clips over your noses to keep the water out and stop you trying to breath in once we are flooded," Scott said, pointing them to some small pincer-like clips attached to their oxygen supply pack.

"Now," he continued, "once the water starts to flow in, place this breathing apparatus, called a Davis Submerged Escape Apparatus, over your face, but only pull it down at the last minute. That rubber tank tied to your chest contains thirty minutes of air. That's more than enough to allow you to undo the escape door and swim to the surface. The small life vest you are wearing will give you buoyancy. When you get out of the hatch, breathe out and keep your arms by your sides. Just kick a bit with your legs. You should shoot to the surface like a cork. Once I open the escape door, we go out in this order – Linda, Jerry, Brian, Cuthbert, and once you're all out, I'll leave last of all. Okay, I'm going to start flooding the tank now."

The two soldiers and two children watched anxiously as water started to pour into the capsule.

"Hey, this water's cold!" Cuthbert cried out in alarm.

"It will be even colder than this if you have to escape from a submarine under the English Channel," the submariner replied. "Now stop talking and get ready to go."

Linda fought to control the fear that was mounting in her. She looked across to Jerry, who seeing the look on her face gave her a reassuring smile. Scott, too, noticed that she looked worried and asked, "Are you all right, my dear?"

Linda nodded and smiled weakly. She knew she could manage as she was determined she would do anything to get back to Jersey.

As the water rose higher, everyone checked their nose clips and put on their goggles and breathing masks.

When the water reached the roof, Scott began to turn a large wheel and then pull the lever to release the escape hatch. After pushing it up to open it fully, he signalled for Linda to go out. As Linda pushed herself out, Jerry was amazed at just how quickly she disappeared from sight.

Next it was Jerry's turn. He remembered his instructions to breathe out as he pushed himself through the hatch. As he did so, he gave his legs a kick and felt himself rising rapidly. He looked up through his goggles. He could see Linda's legs through the water as she rose about ten feet above him. Suddenly Jerry felt himself come to the surface of the water so quickly that he felt he was going to leap right out of it. As he fell back into the tank, Brian, followed by Cuthbert, and lastly Scott all rapidly surfaced next to him. He looked across to Linda who had swum over to the steps and was hanging on to them as she took off her breathing mask.

"Wow!" she exclaimed in excitement. "That was just great. I hope we can do it again. I don't know why I was so worried."

"Me too," Jerry replied after removing the clip from his nose and taking off his mask. "I came up so quickly I never had time to really enjoy myself."

Brian swam across alongside Cuthbert to join them. "Now I really know why I joined the army and not the navy," he said jokingly. "I definitely prefer dry land."

"Well, what did you think?" Commodore Harewood asked as he stood at the top of the ladder, helping the swimmers out of the tank.

"Great!" Linda replied, still smiling.

"Fantastic! Can we do it again, please?" Jerry asked with his usual cheek.

"Sorry, but no," the naval officer answered, "unless you're doing it for real on your way back to Jersey."

"Why would you ever want do that again?" Cuthbert exclaimed. "It was terrifying."

"Now you at least know how to escape from a submarine if something happens to it," the commodore said, "but hopefully everything will be okay for you." He turned to Scott as he climbed out of the tank. "Looks like everything went well, Scott?"

"No problems at all, sir," he replied as he lifted himself off the top rung and stood next to his commanding officer. "I'd give those two youngsters a job in the navy anytime, sir. Linda was a bit nervous but they were expert in the way they left the capsule. As for the two army lads," he continued, without looking in the direction of Brian or Cuthbert, "I think they need a lot more work. Another ten or so practices in this tank should bring them up to scratch with the rest of us. Always takes the army a while to catch on."

Commodore Harewood laughed as he looked from his able seaman towards Brian and Cuthbert.

"What a nerve!" Cuthbert responded, looking directly across at Scott.

"Unfortunately, we will have to walk all the way down ten flights of steps from here," the commodore explained with a smile, looking towards the steep metal staircase he had just climbed, "but just be thankful, because you took the quick way to the top through the water. I had to walk all the way up. Come on, down we go, once you are all dry and dressed we will get you some tea before I explain what we will be doing with you tomorrow."

CHAPTER 18

Next morning the four were roused bright and early at HMS Varbel. The sun had just crept above the horizon and was scattering the darkness away. It looked to be the start of a beautiful day.

"Have you seen the view?" Jerry called to Linda as he banged on the door to her room. "It's one of the most impressive things I have ever seen."

"Hang around, Jerry," Linda called in reply. "I've just washed my hair but won't be a minute."

"Hello there, Jerry," Commodore Harewood said as he rounded the corner of the corridor on the third floor of the hotel. "It looks like it will be a cracking day today for your trip out along the Western Isles to Kylesku. Have you seen the view across Loch Striven?"

"Yes, I have. I was just trying to tell Linda about it. Just look at the hills!"

"I never tire of that view," Commodore Harewood replied, his smile broadening. "I didn't think that I'd like a posting up here to Scotland. However, I think that it's just perfect – quiet, scenic, plenty of fresh air and away from the bombs falling on our cities."

"Good morning, Jerry," Linda said as the door to her room opened and she breezed out, her hair still damp and frizzed up after a vigorous rubbing with a towel.

"Look at the view," Jerry said, pointing across the sea to the distant hills.

"Wow," Linda exclaimed, "and to think that God created all that!"

Commodore Harewood looked at her, a puzzled expression on his face. "Do you really believe that God created it?"

"Yes, I do," Linda replied, still looking out across the sea. "I believe that God designed every single hill and valley that we can see across there."

"You don't believe we came from monkeys, then?"

"I don't."

Brian appeared out of his bedroom and joined the conversation. "You'll not shift these two on what they believe. They became real Christians through reading Jerry's uncle's Bible and it has literally changed their lives."

"Really?" the commodore responded, arching an eyebrow in interest. "You know, when I was just a wee boy growing up in Portsmouth, I was sent every week by my parents to Sunday school. I never really wanted to go, I'd rather have been down at the docks watching the great warships coming and going, but they did teach us a lot about the Bible there."

"I used to go to Sunday school too," Brian added. "I learned a lot there as well. I think I can still remember some of the Bible verses we learned."

"Yes, I can remember some too."

"Which ones can you remember?" Linda asked excitedly.

"Let's see now," Commodore Harewood replied, thinking hard. " 'In the beginning God created the heaven and the earth.' Genesis chapter one and verse one. 'For God so loved the world, that He gave His only begotten Son, that whosoever believeth in Him should not perish, but have everlasting life.' John chapter three and verse sixteen. 'God hath given to us eternal life, and this life is in His Son.' First John chapter five and verse eleven. There you are, three verses I was taught in Sunday school over thirty years ago. Not bad, hey?"

"That was great," Jerry enthused.

"Very impressive," Brian added with a smile.

"What about you, Brian? Which ones do you remember? You did tell us when we first arrived on the Isle of Wight," Linda continued eagerly.

"Oh, no," Brian replied, smiling sheepishly. "Not here. Not now. Maybe later sometime. Anyway, isn't it time we had breakfast? I'm ravenous," he added, trying to change the subject.

Commodore Harewood, keen to continue the conversation, said, "Well, I can remember a song I learned at that Sunday school. In fact, even now I sometimes hum it when I'm in my office."

"How does it go?" Jerry asked.

"Something like this, I think." And to their surprise the commodore actually started to sing.

> *Jesus loves me, this I know,*
> *For the Bible tells me so.*
> *Little ones to Him belong;*
> *They are weak, but He is strong.*

> *Yes, Jesus loves me!*
> *Yes, Jesus loves me!*
> *Yes, Jesus loves me!*
> *The Bible tells me so.*

> *Jesus loves me, He who died*
> *Heaven's gate to open wide.*
> *He can take away my sin,*
> *Let His little child come in.*

> *Yes, Jesus loves me!*
> *Yes, Jesus loves me!*
> *Yes, Jesus loves me!*
> *The Bible tells me so.*

"That's great," Linda said excitedly as the four burst into spontaneous applause.

"You certainly have a lovely singing voice," added Cuthbert, who had been standing in the doorway of his bedroom, listening.

After making their way down the corridor to the canteen, the five of them proceeded towards the hatch to get their various breakfasts of porridge, followed by bacon, eggs, sausages and bread, before sitting down at a table to eat.

"Today we are all going to take a trip around the Western Isles to our base in Kylesku where tomorrow you will receive training in one of our new mini submarines. The journey will take all day and you will be staying in Kylesku tonight. Once your training is complete you will return here, and when we receive the go-ahead from those in authority you will be taken down the River Clyde to Holy Loch, out of which most of the fleet submarines sail. From there, we will hopefully get you two youngsters on a submarine and back home to Jersey and your parents," the commodore explained.

"Excellent," Linda exclaimed. "It all seems to be falling into place. We will be there before the twentieth, won't we?"

"Yes, don't worry. The RN knows exactly when you need to be back."

"What's the RN?" Jerry asked, puzzled.

"It's short for Royal Navy," Brian explained. "Just as RAF is short for Royal Air Force."

"Oh, I see," Jerry replied as he smiled back weakly. "I suppose if I was back at school, listening to Miss Harzo's English class, she would be calling that an abbreviation."

"I guess she would," Cuthbert joined in.

"Hey," said Linda, "do you remember when Martin Jackson squirted that ink at Miss Harzo and stained the back of her dress whilst she was writing on the blackboard? It was so very funny."

"Wasn't it just?" Jerry agreed, his face breaking into a big smile as he remembered. "It wasn't quite so funny for him when he was caught trying the same trick the second time, though."

"Oh, no!" Linda pursed her lips and grimaced in remembrance. "He was caned by Mrs Heibert."

"Poor Martin. I wonder how he's getting on."

"And our other friends. Just imagine if they knew that we were up here in Scotland training to go on a submarine."

"Yes, some might be green with envy," Jerry responded.

"I might be green with seasickness," Cuthbert interjected helpfully, "if we have to travel on a boat up to this place Kyle... What's its name?"

"Kylesku," the commodore added helpfully. "Just remember 'Kyle' and the first part of 'skew-whiff', you know, when something isn't straight, and put them together. Kylesku."

Everything seemed unbelievably well organised. Jerry realised that a lot of effort and expense was going to be made to get them back to Jersey. He wondered again whether there was something more to returning them to Jersey than they had been told. Maybe they would never find out. He pushed the thought to the back of his mind but wondered whether he should ask Cuthbert or Brian.

"So where is this Kylesku place?" Brian enquired. "And how long will it take to get there?"

"It's right on the far north west of Scotland. We will leave straight after breakfast. It is about three hundred and fifty miles, so, as I said to the children, we will be sailing all day to get there, right past and through the Western Isles. At twenty knots, it should take about fifteen hours."

"Three hundred and fifty miles?" Brian questioned in disbelief.

"Fifteen hours on a boat," Cuthbert added, his face creasing into a worried frown.

"Well, it's longer by sea in miles but shorter in time. The roads from here up through the Highlands are pretty dicey and bendy. In any case, we are taking some other lads up with us to start some training, so we have the French ship, *La Capricieuse*, ready to take us."

"I just hope it's not going to be stormy today," said Brian.

"No, the weather forecast is very favourable for the next few days. Today should be dry with sunny spells and a light westerly wind so all should be very calm and pleasant. In fact," he added, turning towards Linda and Jerry, "you nearly always see dolphins and porpoises somewhere on this journey. If we are really lucky you might catch sight of a whale. These wonderful creatures seem to love the waters around the islands on this west coast."

"That would be great," Linda said eagerly. "We don't see those creatures around Jersey."

"I think my dad saw some dolphins once when he was on a fishing boat between Guernsey and Sark, but I have never seen any, so this trip might be fun," Jerry added.

CHAPTER 19

The small motor tender was tied up alongside the ex-French destroyer. The four novices, with the commodore, made their way up a dropdown metal stairway onto the deck of *La Capricieuse.*

"This really is some ship," Jerry stated as he looked round at the gun emplacement mounted high up at the stern. "It's much bigger than I expected."

"This is just a tiny ship compared to the majority that the Royal Navy are using. It was captured from the French in July last year and is really a minesweeper to locate German-laid mines, but its operating here at present. It's ideal for short trips such as ours today."

"Short trips," Cuthbert repeated in alarm. "I do not call three hundred and fifty miles a short trip. I call that a cruise!"

"Ah, here is Captain Metcalf," Commodore Harewood said as a tall, lean, erect gentleman, in an immaculate Royal Navy uniform of dark blue with gold buttons, strode down the deck towards them.

"Good morning, sir," the captain said, looking at Commodore Harewood and saluting him smartly. "Good to have you aboard."

"Good morning, Captain. How's our little trip for today looking?" the commodore asked.

"Just taking on the last few men going to join the X-craft for training and we'll be on the move."

"Good, good. Allow me to introduce my four companions. This is Sergeant Cuthbert Rennoldson and Medical Orderly Brian Oliver from the army, along with Linda De La Haye and Jerry Le Godel, both from Jersey."

"My word," Captain Metcalf exclaimed. "Whatever are you two doing here from Jersey?"

Jerry was just about to launch into his umpteenth explanation of their daring trip, when the commodore answered for him instead.

"It's a long story which I can give you on the way up. I think maybe we had better weigh anchors and start on our way, don't you?"

As the ship got underway and commenced steaming south through Rothesay Bay and out into the Firth of Clyde, Jerry, Linda, Cuthbert and Brian walked around the decks, carefully taking in its various guns and superstructure.

"It really is so big," Jerry repeated as Captain Metcalf came back to see them.

"Well, it is only between six and seven hundred tons and about two hundred and fifty feet long. Some of our largest ships are over forty thousand tons. HMS *Hood*, which was sunk in May, was nearly fifty thousand tons and over eight hundred feet long."

"Amazing." Jerry shook his head in awe.

"Yes, those big ships are some feat of engineering. Anyway, hopefully today should be a good day for us to sail as the weather is fair. If it's rough, this ship really rolls as it has a very shallow bottom. You need a good stomach to sail in her during those conditions."

Cuthbert turned to Brian and said, "Well, we need to be thankful for small mercies, then."

The captain continued, "We will sail down past Millport on our port beam then pass alongside the Isle of Arran on our starboard beam before heading across the bottom of the Campbeltown peninsula and out into the Atlantic Ocean. Then we will head west-north-west before turning again to starboard and heading up the west side of the Inner Hebrides."

"I have never been able to know which is port and which is starboard," Brian said as he looked at the captain.

"Oh, that's easy. Sailors used to drink a lot of Port wine

and the question was often asked, 'Is there any Port left?' If port is left, then starboard must be..."

"Right," Jerry replied without being asked.

"Correct," the captain answered with a chuckle. "I think we could make a seaman out of you yet, Jerry."

"And what is the Inner Hed...er...Hebree...That other place you mentioned?" Linda enquired with her usual enthusiasm.

"The main Western Islands of Scotland are grouped into two parts – the Outer Hebrides, which stand further out into the Atlantic Ocean, are made up of the main islands of Lewis and Harris. The Inner Hebrides are closer to the Scottish mainland and have such islands as Mull, Rum, Eigg, Tiree, Islay and Skye included in their number. You will see as we turn onto a northerly heading that the western seaboard of Scotland is one of the most spectacular in the world."

Jerry looked at Linda. "I'm really looking forward to this trip, aren't you?"

"Yes, I am and it keeps our mind off what might be happening in Jersey. It really is so much more interesting learning about a place by seeing it rather than sitting in some old classroom reading from an old worn-out textbook. I never even knew all these islands existed off Scotland. I hope we see some whales, I really do. That will be great to tell when we finally get back to Jersey."

The two friends spent most of the time standing on deck looking out to sea despite the chilly breeze that continually blew across the ship's deck. Occasionally they would ask someone where they were and what bit of land or mountain range they could see. They enjoyed watching the water as it frothed, foamed and rolled away from the ship's bow, leaving a long wake in the sea behind.

After a few hours of sailing, Linda suddenly called out, "I see something. There! Over there in the water. What is it?"

"Looks like a dirty old football to me," Jerry replied as he too caught sight of the small, round, dark object that Linda had pointed out.

As they watched, another similar dark shape appeared, followed by a third.

"You watching the seals, are you?" a pleasant young sailor in his smart uniform asked.

"So that's what they are," Linda answered as yet another small, round head appeared to join its friends. "I thought that seals would be much bigger than that."

"Well, lassie, you can only see the heads as most of the body is under the water. However, if you saw them up close on land you would be able to see that they are much bigger than they look there," the sailor answered, glad for an opportunity to leave his chores and chat with the two young passengers.

"That's amazing," Jerry responded, still looking out at the heads bobbing about in the water. "I have seen a single seal, off Plemont back home, but never a number like that."

"So where is home?" the sailor asked, leaning against the ship's rails and watching the two as they scanned the sea.

"Jersey," they echoed in unison.

"Jersey?" the sailor announced with almost disbelief. "Jersey?" he again repeated. "But I heard that had been occupied by the Nazis!"

"It has," Jerry replied, looking across to the young man who seemed as if he should still be in school, "but we escaped and came to the Isle of Wight!"

"Why did you do that?" the sailor asked as he turned to face the two.

"Look!" shouted Linda, pointing out to sea at an area of disturbed water. "What was that?"

"I don't see anything," Jerry answered, looking to where Linda was pointing.

"Me neither," the sailor agreed as he too looked at the area of disturbed water.

"I'm sure it was a whale that surfaced," Linda exclaimed, her eyes glued to the spot as the ship moved forward. "There!" she shouted again, pointing to a rapidly disappearing grey mass about one hundred yards from the ship.

"It is a whale," Jerry acknowledged, his face etched in deep concentration as he again began to scan the seascape before him.

"Bit further south than normal," the sailor said nonchalantly. "Usually see them north of Rum. Must be good fishing around today. Can you see that long line of disturbed water over there where the colours change and there are lots of air bubbles? That's where two water currents meet and it usually means lots of fish and therefore a good place to look for seals, dolphins and whales."

"Hey, I never knew that," Jerry enthused, still looking intently across the sea. "I have seen those areas around Jersey but never realised just what they are."

"How would we know if a submarine was around?" Linda suddenly asked the young sailor, changing the subject a little.

"Sonar," he answered confidently.

"What's sonar?" she asked him.

"It, er, sort of picks up noises under the water," he explained. "Noises like engines and such like. We would know if a submarine of any shape or size was nearby because our sonar operator would pick up the sound travelling through the water."

"That's amazing," Linda smiled. "It's just a pity it cannot tell us where the whales and dolphins are."

Several hours later, as they were all having supper together with the captain in his quarters, Cuthbert spoke up.

"I've been cruising all day with the Royal Navy in order to be trained for life on a submarine, but what I can't understand is why we couldn't do all this in Portsmouth. Why do we have to come to this Kyle stew place?"

"The place is Kylesku," Captain Metcalf responded, "and we go there because it's a great place, well away from German bombers, not easily found either by air or by spies and has plenty of challenging sea waters through which to navigate a small submarine. Not to mention that its geology is similar to that in some of the places where we might be working in the future."

"Oh, I see," Cuthbert replied, giving a short smile as if to acknowledge that he had understood everything. "I guess that using somewhere like Portsmouth might be bit dangerous, especially with the Germans bombing it regularly."

"Did I hear you explaining why we are using Kylesku?" Commodore Harewood enquired amiably as he joined them for supper.

"Yes, sir, I was," Captain Metcalf replied, straightening up at the voice of his commanding officer.

"It provides plenty of challenges for submarine use with deep, narrow passages, a large tidal bay called Eddrachillis Bay and access to a couple of inland sea lochs which lie beyond Kylesku. It really couldn't be better for our requirements," the commodore added as he took over the explanation from the captain.

"The commodore likes Kylesku so much he has even learnt a song about the place and often sings it whilst playing his piano accordion," Captain Metcalf butted in with a slight twinkle in his eye.

"Really?" said Linda with enthusiasm. "Oh, do please sing it for us. You have such a lovely singing voice."

"Ah, well. Despite your lovely invitation, young Linda, I'm happy to report that I will be unable to sing the requested song because I have not brought my accordion with me," Commodore Harewood answered with a wry smile.

"Oh, that's not a problem," the captain responded, seemingly just as anxious to hear his commodore sing. "Able Seaman Fletcher has one in the mess room. I'll send him for it."

Fifteen minutes later, Commodore Harewood, with piano accordion strapped across his chest, was giving a masterful recital to an appreciative audience made up of two army lads, two young people, a navy captain and a few ratings who had managed to incorporate duties to allow them to hear the commodore sing in the sailors' mess room.

By Clebrig and Ben Loyal and the bonnie Kyle of Tongue
The roads we oft times travelled in the days when we were
*   young*
There's magic and there's beauty in those Hills while passing
*   through*
There's many a mile from Melness to the Waters of Kylesku.

O'er all of Bonnie Scotland, I dearly love the west
Its bens and glens in summer time they surely are the best
There's grandeur and there's beauty in those Hills while
*   passing through*
There's many a mile from Lairg to the Waters of Kylesku.

By Craggie pool and Loyal and the Coldbackie sands
I've thought of them while soldiering in far-off foreign lands
I dreamt I saw the sunset o'er the hills of Casheldhu
In fancy I was wandering by the Waters of Kylesku.

As the haunting melody of the music from the accordion died away and Commodore Harewood's voice fell silent, Jerry and Linda were the first to lead the applause with enthusiastic clapping and a few 'whoops' from Jerry for good measure. The sailors who had gathered round the door and along the passageway also joined in approvingly until Captain Metcalf gave them a knowing look that said, 'Show over, back to work!'

Commodore Harewood also caught sight of the captain's look and added playfully to those standing around, "Back to your stations or I'll string you all up from the highest yardarm and then make you all walk the plank!"

CHAPTER 20

After a safe arrival in Kylesku and a good night's sleep in a crofter's cottage close to the submarine training base, Jerry and Linda awoke to another bright and clear day. They stepped out of the little cottage and gazed around them at the spectacular sight. Behind the cottage, mountains rose hundreds of feet and, in front, a narrow passage of crystal clear water stretched out into the distance before widening into a large bay. The clear blue sky was reflected in the water and the rising sun glinted on it as it caught the ripples of the small waves that broke over the shore.

"It's just as beautiful as home," Linda whispered to Jerry in an awestruck tone.

"I agree," Jerry replied, "but it's an awful lot colder. That is a real cold breeze that's blowing."

"That's because we are nearly at the top of Scotland," Commodore Harewood replied as he came into view round the corner of the cottage. "I would say that we are over six hundred miles further north than Jersey here at Kylesku so it will be much cooler. And that water might look inviting, but don't try swimming in it as it's freezing even in the height of summer. Right, come on, let's get those two army boys into action stations then we'll have some breakfast at the base and get you lot trained up for travelling in a submarine."

After consuming a hearty breakfast of bacon, egg, sausages, fried bread and toast, Jerry and Linda, accompanied by their two army charges and the commodore, boarded a small motorboat that took them across to the other side of the water. The smallest submarine Jerry could ever have imagined stood moored alongside a small jetty.

"We are not going on that, are we?" Cuthbert exclaimed, looking between the submarine and the commodore. "Please tell me we are not going on that!"

"No, Sergeant," the commodore replied casually, "you will not be going *on* it. The intention is for you to travel *in* it. You see, if you're inside you will stay much drier."

Cuthbert groaned and looked in consternation at the small craft now sitting just in front of the motorboat. It was only about fifty feet long and around six feet wide.

"Why doesn't it have a large bit on top in the middle?" Jerry asked, recalling pictures of submarines he had seen in books.

"You mean a conning tower," the commodore smiled. "Well, this is designed to be small and agile and to go anywhere, and a conning tower, or as you put it 'a large bit on top in the middle', would make it harder to negotiate small inlets, lochs and fjords."

"All four of us will never fit in that," Brian stated, echoing Cuthbert's thoughts.

"Oh, you will, you will, plus another two crew members who operate the submarine," Commodore Harewood answered, smiling at the obvious fear that was possessing the two army men. "But don't worry, we will split you up when it goes out on its practise drill."

"But...but...but," Cuthbert stammered, still looking at the small submarine before him, "you don't seriously intend us to travel to Jersey in something that small, do you?"

"Oh, no, not at all," the commodore replied. "This one is just for practice. What you travel in to Jersey will be much bigger."

"Well, I'm keen to get inside and find out what it is really like to be in a submarine," Jerry enthused as he stepped from the launch onto the jetty next to the tiny submarine. "It's almost like a large toy that someone would have built for the Battle of Flowers back home, don't you think, Linda?"

"Yes, I suppose I could see it on one of those floats covered in carnations and dahlias," Linda agreed, joining her friend on the jetty.

"Whatever is the Battle of Flowers?" Cuthbert asked as he joined them on the wooden jetty.

"Oh, it's a parade that we hold every year in Jersey. It started at the beginning of the century, I think, to commemorate someone becoming king and has sort of continued from there," Jerry explained as he continued to look down with interest at the submarine lying in the water before him.

"It was for King Edward the Seventh's coronation." Linda thought she had better give a bit more of an explanation. "Now each parish makes a display from flowers and tries to outdo the others in making the biggest, best, most colourful display."

Jerry butted in, while still surveying the submarine, "Then at the end of the parade they pull all the flowers off the displays and throw them at each other, which is why we call it the Battle of Flowers."

"Um, I see," Commodore Harewood replied. "If only this war was a case of us throwing flowers at one another. Come on, let's show you around this contraption."

All four cautiously stepped from the jetty to join the two crew members standing on the narrow deck of the strange craft.

"Right, it is going to be quite a squeeze, as it is only built for four, but I'll show you all round first and then Able Seamen Clark and Davis here will take you out in two trips and do a few manoeuvres out in the bay. That way you will get used to being in a confined space and being under the water."

With care, the four followed the commodore through the vertical hatch into the submarine and then through another horizontal metalled door hatch that led into the cramped confines of the submarine's control room.

"I never knew they could make these so small," Brian commented as he squeezed himself into a tight corner surrounded by small wheels and dials of various sizes. "Not even Jerry and Linda can stand upright in this!"

"This is the only one," Commodore Harewood explained. "It's a training vessel. As I said, if you can cope in here, you can cope in anything. It is very small and really only made for four people. Any more than that would tax its oxygen supply and also make trying to pilot it extremely difficult and hazardous." Pointing at a series of pipes that led to various gauges, he went on to explain, "All these are dials which indicate depth, speed, oxygen levels and also show which tanks have been flooded or blown. The larger wheel over there is the helm which steers the craft, whether on the surface or underwater. If there is anything else you want to know, speak to Clark and Davis when they take you out. Now, I was going to pair you up one youngster and one soldier, however, I've changed my mind. I think that you, Jerry and Linda, should stay together, so you'll go out first and then Cuthbert and Brian."

"Great," Jerry enthused. "This is exciting. I'm glad we're first."

"I think I'd call it terrifying!" Cuthbert mumbled just loud enough for everyone to hear. "The problem is that Jerry and Linda always seem to find extra adventures which we are not looking for. I'm sure something will happen that no one was expecting."

Jerry and Linda stayed aboard the submarine whilst the commodore led the two soldiers out of the hatch and back to the jetty.

"Hi! My name's Alex and this is George," introduced one of the sailors as he pulled the hatch shut and spun the wheel to tighten and seal it. "We gather you two have already been through some daring escapades."

The submarine was soon on its way with Able Seaman Alex Davis taking control of the helm whilst Able Seaman George Clark rotated several dials, pulled levers and checked gauges.

"How do you know where you are going?" Linda suddenly enquired as she realised for the first time that there were no windows. "I mean, won't we bump into something if we can't see anything?"

"Oh, Linda," Jerry replied in exasperation. "Submarines have a thing that sticks up through the water, called a stethoscope, that allows the crew to see which way they are travelling."

"It's a periscope, actually," George corrected Jerry, smiling broadly. "I believe a stethoscope is what doctors use to examine your chest."

Linda giggled with delight at Jerry's mistake. "Oh, well," Jerry replied, feeling a bit deflated and embarrassed. "I knew it was some sort of scope anyway."

After about fifteen minutes, Alex said, "Prepare to dive." George pulled two levers above his head. Alex added, "Okay, dive, dive, dive, full ahead group down."

Both youngsters watched intrigued as the two submariners pushed, pulled and twiddled levers to make the submarine comply with their wishes.

"Okay, half ahead group down," Alex requested as George twiddled yet another small knob. It all sounded like a totally different language to Jerry and Linda as they continued to watch, enthralled by all they were seeing and hearing.

"Periscope depth," Alex commanded. "Ten feet."

"Periscope depth it is," George replied as he raised a small cylindrical tube with what looked like a pair of binoculars on the bottom. After swinging round with the binocular type thing pressed tightly to his eyes he pulled away and enquired, "Would you like to take a look?"

"Yes, please," both youngsters echoed almost in unison.

Jerry was desperate to look out but knew that he had to let Linda take first turn, and having already made the mistake of calling the periscope a stethoscope, he was not keen to embarrass himself further by rushing in front of Linda.

"Oh," Linda said slowly as she looked into the eyepiece and began to swing it round. "That's amazing. Would anyone on the surface of the sea be able to see us or know that we are here?"

"Only if they were very lucky and were looking at the place where the periscope sticks out of the sea," George answered. "With there being so much water and as it is constantly moving, it would be incredibly hard to see."

When it was his turn, Jerry eagerly took the periscope handles and pressed his eyes close to it. "Wow! That is so clear. You can see all the way round through one hundred and eighty degrees!"

"You can actually see round three hundred and sixty degrees," George corrected him.

"Um, yes, er, that's what I meant," Jerry replied, embarrassed for the second time. "Sums and things were never my strong points."

"Jerry," Linda scolded, trying to imitate one of their school teachers. "How many times do I have to remind you to only comment on things you know something about?"

Jerry smiled sheepishly as both George and Alex continued to guide the submarine through its various manoeuvres.

CHAPTER 21

"Let's drop a little deeper," Alex said, reading the compass in front of him and the depth gauge situated high to his left. "Flood Q."

"Q flooding," George replied as he pulled on yet another small lever.

"How deep can these little submarines go?" Linda enquired as the craft commenced dropping at a slight angle further into the deep, dark waters of Eddrachillis Bay.

"Well, we have tested this one to around three hundred feet, but it was groaning a bit at that depth," Alex answered.

"Groaning?" Jerry frowned at Alex in the light cast from the electric lamps situated in the roof of the submarine.

"Yes, the deeper we go, the more the water pressure builds up outside the hull. If we go too deep it would crush the submarine and we would all be killed," Alex explained. "We don't actually measure the depth of water in feet. We use a term called 'fathoms' where one fathom equates to six feet. So at three hundred feet depth we would say we were at fifty fathoms."

"Oh," Jerry responded, rather perplexed by the nautical terminology.

"Anyway, here the water is about one hundred and fifty feet, so we will just dive down and sit on the bottom for a few minutes before surfacing," George added, giving details of their next manoeuvre.

Eventually the occupants felt the submarine gently rest on the shingle bed of the sea.

"Stop motors. Silent routine," Alex commanded.

"What is a silent routine?" Linda asked.

"It's when we all stay silent, say, for instance, in the event of an attack by an enemy ship. Because they can't see, they have to guess where we are. If they have sonar they will be listening in to try to discover our position so that they can depth charge us more accurately. So if we stay on the bottom and remain completely silent, they may think we have gone away," Alex tried to explain.

"I hadn't thought that we could be depth charged on our way home," Jerry commented, twitching his nose nervously.

"Time to surface, I think," George said, looking at his watch.

"Right you are," Alex replied.

"Stand by to surface," George commanded. "Shut main vents."

"Main vents shut," Alex confirmed.

When nothing happened, both submariners looked at each other and then the children in alarm.

"Are you sure the vents are shut?" George asked.

"Yes, quite sure," his colleague replied, still looking worried.

"Blow the tanks," George ordered.

Alex pushed at a couple of levers and twiddled a couple of wheels but nothing happened.

"Are we stuck?" Linda asked, trying to suppress a slight feeling of panic that had been building ever since she saw the look of concern on the faces of the two sailors.

"Well...it's not looking good just at present," George replied, slowly tapping a dial and peering at the needle behind the glass. "I've never known this before. It seems that nothing is responding to anything we do."

"Then will the others come and rescue us?" Jerry enquired, also feeling a little nervous.

"Do you think they have a line and a big hook to drop down and sort of fish us out?" George said with a wry smile. "No, if we can't get this thing to respond we have to bail out using the Davis Submerged Escape Apparatus. You should have been instructed about that before you came up here."

"You mean in the escape tank?" Jerry clarified.

"That's the one," Alex replied. "Except the water here will be ten times colder than in that tank, and we are a lot deeper. The gauge says twenty-six fathoms and that's just under one hundred and sixty feet."

"Can we escape safely from this depth?" Linda asked, the feeling of panic starting to show on her face.

"Yes, we can escape, but it will be dark and very cold, and it will seem that you will never reach the surface. It's a bit different in real life than in the Submarine Escape Training Tank."

Jerry looked across at Linda and saw the worried frown on her face. "Don't worry, Linda," he encouraged, looking directly at her. "Just remember the times that God has already saved and protected us. When the Germans captured Uncle Fred in Guernsey, no German soldier looked down that cliff face to see us. Then when the engine broke down, God sent the wind to blow us up the English Channel, and when we landed in the storm and on the beach laid with mines, He kept us safe. He'll do the same for us now. I know He will!"

"So you believe in God, do you?" George enquired easily.

"Yes, we became Christians after reading my uncle's Bible in the boat on the way from Jersey through the English Channel."

"I see. So are you saved?" Alex asked.

"What do you mean?" Jerry replied, looking puzzled.

"I had a friend who became a Christian and he always used to say he was saved. 'Saved from sin and saved from hell.' That's what he used to say," Alex explained.

"Yes, I guess we are saved, if that's what being saved means," Jerry replied. "Tell me again what your friend used to say."

"Saved from sin and saved from hell."

"Well, do you think we can save ourselves from being stuck down here?" George asked, as he handed Jerry and Linda the Davis Submerged Escape Apparatus. Here, you know how to put this on. There really is no point in us waiting down here if nothing is working. The sooner we get out the better."

In just over a minute, all four sat in the cramped submarine wearing their breathing and buoyancy aids. "Now, remember," Alex instructed, "don't move until this place is completely flooded. Then George will open the escape hatch and get out first so that he can help you two out. Once you're both out, I'll follow and we will surface together to ensure we are all safe. Understand?"

The terrified youngsters nodded. They had enjoyed the practice in the escape tank but this was different. They were stuck in a real submarine more than one hundred and fifty feet below sea level in freezing water where the only way out was to flood the craft and swim up to the surface.

Suddenly, Alex removed his mask and goggles and smiled at them. "Okay, the exercise is over. We are not really stuck, but just checking to see how you'd both react if we were. I must say I am most impressed with how calm you both stayed."

Jerry and Linda looked at each other with relief as they removed their goggles and air tanks.

"You know, many prospective submariners who we train are all right until we tell them we are trapped. Sometimes we have nearly had fights down here, they have been so terrified," George explained. "I must say, though, I almost wondered if you had worked out that we were kidding you as you were so calm."

"If you had seen me inside, I was all churned up and almost ready to cry," Linda replied, her face breaking into a smile of relief.

"Me too," Jerry replied. " I was trying to remember a Bible verse that my uncle read to us the day we left Jersey that came true twice for us afterwards. It went sort of like this, 'When thou passest through the waters, I will be with thee, when thou walkest through the fire, thou shalt not be burned.' "

"All right, let's go up," Alex said. "Start engines." A slight whining noise came through the submarine and was accompanied by a familiar slight vibration. "Blow main tanks."

George pushed two levers on the roof forward and the children felt themselves rising gently off the seabed.

"Full ahead group up," Alex commanded as they moved quicker at an upward angle. "Shut number one Kingston."

"Number one Kingston shut," George replied like an echo.

"Stand by to surface...surfacing."

Jerry and Linda felt the submarine stop rising and almost fall back as it broke out of the water.

"We're on the surface," Alex said casually. "I'll open the hatch to let in some fresh air."

Neither Jerry nor Linda admitted to either of their companions in the submarine, but they were mighty glad to see the rays of sun streaming through the entrance hatch and feel the breeze of fresh air.

"Oh, that looks and feels great," Linda said as she pulled herself onto the narrow deck.

"I must say that you had me rather worried down there when you said we were stuck," Jerry confessed, smiling nervously as he joined Linda on the deck.

"Well, just take a few more good lungfuls of air and we'll get back inside, head to the jetty and then take your army pals out," George said as he looked back across to the land and the jetty about two miles away.

Jerry and Linda watched as Alex pulled the hatch door shut and secured it by pulling a metal lever across.

"We'll dive to periscope depth and make for home," George said, taking the helm.

"How deep is periscope depth?" Jerry enquired.

"About ten feet or thereabouts," George answered. "It's no good for clear water as we would be seen below the surface, but we are almost totally invisible in most normal conditions."

"Stand by to flood W," George said to Alex who was squatting nearer the rear of the submarine. "Okay, flood W. Slow ahead group down. Diving!"

"Periscope depth," Alex said, looking at a dial that said 'depth gauge' in small writing behind the glass.

"Periscope depth," George repeated after a few seconds.

Alex took a small button on a short lead leaning against the hull of the craft and gave it a press. The periscope moved up from the floor and as it did so he pulled two handles down and commenced to peer through it, swinging it around to get a good look. Suddenly, he took a sharp intake of breath and exclaimed, "Crash dive, quickly!" As he said the words, he closed up the two handles on the periscope and pushed it with urgent force to its resting place on the floor.

George immediately pushed two levers forward and the submarine began to fall through the sea at a rapid rate, twisting from one side to another.

"What's the matter?" Jerry asked, not sure whether this was another hoax or not.

"Just hold on tight," Alex shouted above the din of escaping air and creaking metal. The small submarine continued on what seemed to Jerry and Linda a crazy, out-of-control motion.

Whatever it was, Jerry and Linda knew that it had to be serious.

CHAPTER 22

As the tiny submarine bucked and kicked on its rapid descent through the sea, Jerry, Linda, Alex and George held on for dear life. Jerry and Linda could feel their stomachs churning from the violent rocking motion and also from their great fear.

Suddenly, George seemed to regain control and said, "Slow group down, gently, gently!"

The submarine started to level out and then there was a gentle bump as it landed on the shingle seabed.

"I feel sick," Jerry said, trying hard to keep his stomach under control.

"What happened?" Linda's voice quivered with fear.

"Well..." George answered, looking round at them, "we had to ensure you could cope in the event of a crash dive and once again you both survived pretty well."

"I'm not sure that I did," Jerry observed, still holding his stomach. "I feel totally sick."

"You mean it was all put on?" Linda asked, still in a state of shock.

"Yes, indeed it was. We are sorry that we had to put you through that but we were just following Commodore Harewood's orders," Alex explained as gently as he could.

"And I thought the commodore was our friend," Jerry mumbled, still feeling as if he could throw up at any moment.

"Oh, I'm sure he is. We have to put all personnel that are going to travel on any submarine through such procedures. It ensures that they are fully prepared if they ever have to do it for real." George pulled another lever. "Blow main ballast. Slow ahead group up," he added as the submarine left the seafloor and commenced yet another trip to the surface.

"Now don't you go telling your army pals about what we have just done, will you?" Alex asked seriously. "We have to do the same manoeuvres with them as we did with you and it's not as effective if they know beforehand."

"No, we won't tell." Linda smiled as she felt the submarine breach the surface of the sea once again.

"I think one look at me and they'll know full well that they are in for a hard time with you two," Jerry added.

"I think we had better open the hatch again and let you have some fresh air," George said, looking with concern at Jerry.

As they stepped off the deck and back onto the jetty, both Linda and Jerry were secretly mightily relieved to be out of the submarine. Despite the best efforts of Cuthbert and Brian to gain some insight as to what it was like, neither youngster gave the game away to the two soldiers.

Three hours later, two weary and pale soldiers walked into the small canteen at the Kylesku naval base. To anyone looking at them it was obvious that they had had a rough time.

"Are those two guys in that thing fully qualified to operate it?" Cuthbert asked Commodore Harewood as he pulled up a chair to the table to join Jerry, Linda and the commodore.

"Yes," the commodore answered with a straight face. "Able Seamen Clark and Davis are the best we have. In fact, they are both in line for promotion."

"Promotion!" Cuthbert barked back in almost total disgust. "Promotion!" he repeated. "The way they treated us they should be drummed out of the navy!"

"Oh, come now, I'm sure that it wasn't that bad," the commodore replied reassuringly.

"Not that bad! Not that bad? Do you know what they did? Made us think we were stuck on the seabed and made us put on those Davis thingamabobs telling us we were going to have to escape through the hatch and swim to the surface."

"Just normal training procedure," the commodore said calmly.

"Yeah, we got stuck on the bottom and we also did a crash dive," Jerry replied.

"Well, weren't you terrified?" Cuthbert replied, looking for the first time at his two young charges.

"Well, we were, just a little," Linda replied mischievously, "but we had a very interesting conversation at the bottom of the sea. We talked about being saved and not just about being saved from the bottom of the sea, but about being saved from sin and hell."

"So while you were in that tiny underwater coffin at the bottom of the sea you were holding a Sunday school? That sounds just about right for these two, doesn't it, Brian?" Cuthbert commented as he looked mischievously across at his still pale-faced friend.

"Well, no, not exactly," Jerry added. "Alex was just explaining that he had a friend who was a Christian and said that he was saved, so Linda and I decided that we must be saved. In fact, I think I remember reading that word somewhere in Uncle Fred's Bible."

"You know, that rings a bell with me," Brian answered, rubbing his chin as if trying to recall something important. "When I was in Sunday school, every year we had to memorise certain Bible verses and they always had a theme."

"You told us all the times the Lord Jesus said 'I Am', just after we landed on the Isle of Wight," Linda reminded him.

"So I did," Brian answered, still wearing a distant look on his face. "But I also remember one year learning some verses that had that word 'saved' in them."

"Can you still remember any of them?" Linda asked excitedly.

"I'm not sure that I could, but let's see now," Brian replied, still with a faraway expression as if he was searching for inspiration. "Here goes, 'Whosoever shall call upon the name of the Lord shall be saved.' Romans chapter ten and verse thirteen, also in Acts chapter two and verse twenty-one.

" 'For God sent not His Son into the world to condemn the world; but that the world through Him might be saved.' John chapter three and verse seventeen.

" 'I am the door: by Me if any man enter in, He shall be saved.' John chapter ten and verse nine. Um, er..." He paused, thinking hard. "I used to be able to say them all without any problem. Oh, yes, and this is how the next one goes – 'God our Saviour, who will have all men to be saved, and to come unto the knowledge of the truth.' First Timothy chapter two, part of verse three, and verse four.

"And the last one that I can remember is 'What must I do to be saved? Believe on the Lord Jesus Christ and thou shalt be saved.' Acts chapter sixteen, verses thirty and thirty-one."

"Well done, indeed," Commodore Harewood enthused. "You know, I was taught that verse about the Lord Jesus being the door to heaven and the only door to heaven. I think there were two little songs we sang about the door too."

"Oh, please sing them to us," Linda pleaded with him.

"Oh, all right, but just let me borrow that accordion to help me as it's been a long time."

As he returned, Commodore Harewood slung the straps of the accordion across his shoulders and gave it a couple of shakes until it was in the position that he wanted. After a couple of practice notes and squeezes of the bellows, he started to sing along.

One door and only one,
And yet its sides are two,
Inside and outside,
On which side are you?

One door and only one,
And yet its sides are two,
I'm on the inside,
On which side are you?

"This is the other song, it's a bit slower."

I am the door,
I am the door,
By Me if any man enter in
He shall be saved,
She shall be saved,
We shall be saved.

I am the door,
The words are but four,
Millions are in
But there's room for more.
The door's open wide,
Come right inside
And thou shalt be saved.

Jerry and Linda clapped enthusiastically as the music on the accordion died away. The commodore closed it up and clipped a little leather strap across it to hold it in place.

"That was brilliant," Linda exclaimed. "You really are in the wrong job. You should have been a singer!"

"Well, thank you, Linda," the commodore smiled. "If I ever become famous as the Crooning Commodore, I'll know that you were my first ever fan."

"What does 'crooning' mean?" Jerry asked.

"It means to sing in a sort of soft or easy style," Brian answered.

"Oh. I hadn't heard that expression before. I just thought that singing was singing," Jerry replied.

"Brian, Commodore," Linda suddenly enquired seriously, "have you ever entered in?"

"I beg your pardon?" the commodore asked, surprised at the sudden question.

"Have you ever entered in?" Linda repeated. "You were singing about the Lord Jesus being the door and you having to enter in. Have you? Are you saved?"

"Oh, er, no. I never did. I sort of thought I'd get it sorted out when I was older."

"Well, you're much older than us, and Jerry and I are both Christians, so what's stopping you?" Linda pressed.

"And we are both saved," Jerry added.

"Maybe when the war is over, then I'll get saved and ready for heaven," the commodore added, feeling most uncomfortable at the interrogation.

"But what if you die during the war?" Jerry added.

"Well, er, I guess I have no answer to that one," Commodore Harewood replied with honesty.

"We had to work out just what God was trying to say to us through the Bible," Linda explained, "and once we saw what the Lord Jesus meant when He said 'I am the way' we just believed it and trusted Him as our Saviour. I just cannot believe that you, and you, Brian, have gone to Sunday school and learnt so much but never trusted Him and become Christians."

"Well," Commodore Harewood said in exasperation, "let's talk about this another time, shall we? Tomorrow we sail back to Bute and the following day you travel to Holy Loch where we intend putting you on a submarine that will take you to Jersey. So there is a lot to do and arrange."

CHAPTER 23

Two days later, Linda, Jerry, Cuthbert and Brian, having sailed back to the Isle of Bute, eventually arrived at Holy Loch. They were tired and weary but ready for the next dangerous part of the operation to return the two brave youngsters to Jersey. Captain Lewis had travelled up from Portsmouth to meet them and greeted them enthusiastically as they stepped onto the deck of HMS *Forth*, a submarine supply ship.

"Well, are you all trained up in the use of submarines?" he enquired with a jovial air. "Commodore Harewood tells me you all did very well in training, with a mention in dispatches for Linda and Jerry for outstanding calmness in the midst of great peril."

"What do you mean that we were 'mentioned in dispatches'?" Jerry enquired, looking bemused.

"Oh, that simply means a commanding officer has written a report, usually to one of his superiors, commending someone's gallant actions. Unfortunately he did not even mention Sergeant Rennoldson or Corporal Oliver." The captain glanced at the two army men with a wry smile. "Oh, yes," the captain added, smiling, "Commodore Harewood also said that you like good singing and that I have to be careful because you might try to coerce me into becoming a Christian."

Linda laughed. "Trust the commodore to say that. You know, he was such a nice man. He sang some lovely songs about the Lord Jesus and quoted some Bible verses that he had learned at Sunday school, but he wasn't a Christian. I cannot understand that."

"Well, I don't know how you can say that Commodore Harewood isn't a Christian. He is one of the finest men I know, and anyway, aren't we are all Christians? Great Britain is a Christian country," the captain replied.

"Watch out, now," Brian added with a smile, looking at the captain. "You may have taken on far more than you can possibly cope with."

"Well, that's not what the Bible says," Jerry said, rummaging in his small bag for his uncle's Bible. He thumbed through its pages trying to find a passage that would show the captain he was wrong.

Linda came to his rescue. "If we are Christians because we live in a Christian county or were born Christians, why did God send the Lord Jesus from heaven and why did He have to die on a cross?"

"Um, er, well, um, I've never really thought about it like that," Captain Lewis stammered. "Obviously the commodore was right in saying that you'd try to get me to become a Christian, and I already thought that I was one. Well, we could discuss these things later. For now, the important thing is getting you two back to Jersey in one piece."

Captain Lewis took them to look at a noticeboard hanging on the side of the large cabin where they were sitting. He tapped a pencil lightly on a map attached to the wall with drawing pins and then moved across to a large sheet of paper that appeared to have a list of names, times and dates written on it. There also seemed to be a lot of handwritten crossings out and changes scribbled here and there. "I think you will be travelling on HMS *Tuna* to return back home. It has arrived in from a patrol in the Bay of Biscay and is not due out again until the middle of next month. As it would have passed the Channel Islands to get to and from Biscay, the crew will have had a bit of experience of that area. We will assemble those who are not away on leave, I'll take command and we will get you home in the next few days."

"Have you heard anything more from our parents?" Linda asked tentatively.

Captain Lewis looked up from his piece of paper. "As far as we know, all is well. The German authorities are keeping to their promise and giving you until the twentieth to get back to Jersey. It's the fourteenth today, so that gives us six full days. That should be plenty of time."

"HMS *Tuna*! They could have given us a submarine with a more noble name than that to return these two to Jersey. In fact, it just sounds a bit fishy, if you ask me," Cuthbert mumbled to Brian.

Captain Lewis looked across at him, "Well, it's the only sub that's available right now and as the orders to get these two youngsters home to Jersey have come from the prime minister himself at Downing Street, we have no choice but to obey. You army fellows can be so awkward at times. You cannot just pick and choose the sub you go on, you know, just because you don't like its name, shape, size or colour scheme."

Cuthbert sighed, rolled his eyes and apologised, looking rather uncomfortable.

"Oh, come on, Cuthbert. It won't be that bad," Brian consoled. "These boys in the navy know what they are doing, just like we do in the army. They know how to drive these submarines so we should be safe with them. Anyway, just think of the awful publicity that the navy would receive if they drowned two important army personnel and two young people."

Cuthbert smiled pathetically. It was clear that he really had no desire to travel under the water again.

Two hours later, the four of them were boarding a submarine that was very much larger than the tiny one they had been training in.

"This is huge," Jerry said as he looked in admiration along the full length of the big grey submarine that lay at berth alongside HMS *Forth*. "I never knew they were so big!"

"This is a T-class submarine and was built here on the River Clyde," Captain Lewis explained as they stepped onto the submarine's deck plating. "It is just short of three hundred feet in length and weighs just over one thousand tons. It is a lot bigger than the small training craft you used up in Kylesku."

"It certainly is a lot bigger," Linda echoed as she too took in the size of HMS *Tuna*, "and, Jerry, look, it has one of those tall bits built onto it that was missing from the little submarine."

"Ah, you mean its conning tower," Captain Lewis responded as he led the way along the deck towards a large tower that looked to the youngsters like a large grey chimney sitting halfway along the length of the submarine.

"Is that the submarine's main control room?" Jerry enquired.

"Oh, no. The control room sits just underneath, right in the middle of the sub. We call it 'amidships'. The control room has the boat's radio, as well as most of the various controls for steering, diving and surfacing. The conning tower houses the sub's periscope and has a watertight compartment that can be used if emergency escape is required," the captain explained.

"I thought the Royal Navy preferred to call their vessels 'ships', not 'boats'," Cuthbert chipped in.

"You are absolutely correct," the captain responded, "all except submarines which we call either submarines, boats, or subs."

"Oh," Cuthbert said. "Well, in the army a tank is a tank and it all seems much simpler."

Once they had all climbed down into the submarine, Captain Lewis pointed out the hundreds of dials, pipes, levers and gauges.

"I thought when I looked on the outside that this would be so much bigger inside, but it's actually very tight on space," Brian announced in surprise.

"It is still much larger than the little thing we were on the other day," Cuthbert said.

"Those are a bit small. However, we always think that if you can cope in one of those you can manage in one of these bigger vessels," Captain Lewis continued. "This will carry a crew of nearly sixty, so it has to be large enough to accommodate them all and allow them space to work effectively. The sub also has to be small enough to work well both on the surface and underwater."

"It's amazing," Jerry breathed, still gazing in awe at the various piping that seemed to dominate the interior.

"Well, we hope to leave Holy Loch just after lunch in order to try to get you two home to Jersey tomorrow night."

"I can't wait," Linda enthused excitedly. "It will be so wonderful to see mum and dad again and stop anything terrible happening."

"It's not going to be that straightforward, you know," the captain cautioned them, dampening their enthusiasm a little. "There are still many dangers to overcome before you land safely on Jersey's shores. But we will do everything we can to get you as close as possible to the cliffs on the North Coast. I am told that you two would know the right place to attempt a landing and for you to scale the cliffs?"

"We know one or two places that we can maybe get up without too much difficulty," Linda replied with a disarming smile. "When we left Jersey, the Germans had not put any mines anywhere on the North Coast cliffs, so hopefully it will just be a case of scrambling up some gorse-covered gullies."

"We just have to hope and pray that no eagle-eyed sentries are looking out over those cliffs through the night. It should be the dark of the moon so there won't be any natural light that could allow us to be seen. Oh, this is an awful war!" the captain finished.

"Don't worry, captain," Jerry replied. "We managed to escape from Jersey in a small, open boat and somehow sail it right up the English Channel, so hopefully we should have no problems getting back with both the navy and army on hand to help."

"Now, don't you be counting upon much help from us army chaps," Cuthbert said with a chuckle. "We promised to come along for the ride just because our superiors thought you might like some familiar faces around. If I'd have known that it also meant travelling in a submarine into enemy territory, I would most certainly have had second thoughts."

"Oh, you wouldn't have just left us?" Jerry replied, enjoying the fun. "I mean, you have been with us since we arrived in July, so you couldn't have abandoned us just like that?"

"Couldn't I?" Cuthbert said, jutting out his jaw. "I'd have had no difficulty whatsoever if it meant not sailing in this big grey monster."

"You are welcome to leave anytime you like," Captain Lewis replied. "We can easily arrange to get you to Glasgow and on a train back south tonight, if you wish?"

"Ah, um, er, well, you see," Cuthbert stuttered and stumbled. "You see, well I-I've sort of come this far, so I guess that I had better just stick it out till the end. I mean, I have sort of grown rather fond of my two young friends."

CHAPTER 24

As the diesel motors of the submarine started up, they sent a vibration right through the boat that brought both fear and comfort to the four extra passengers on this special voyage. Captain Lewis had taken command himself and organised a crew of men, most of whom had volunteered for the extra trip despite being home on leave. The submarine pulled away from its supply ship and commenced on its way out of Holy Loch and into the River Clyde.

"We will be travelling down through the North Channel between Scotland and Northern Ireland, then on into the Irish Sea," Captain Lewis explained.

"Will we be submerged or on the surface?" Brian asked.

"On the surface, until we round Land's End and head out into the English Channel, then we will dive to avoid being seen by any enemy ships or planes. *Tuna* uses much less diesel when sailing on the surface so we will stay topside for as far as we dare."

"Well, that's the most sensible thing that I have heard anyone in the navy say so far," Cuthbert added in a concerned voice. "I just don't like this idea of being under the water at all. If the Good Lord had intended me to go underwater, He'd have given me flippers."

"You would suit them," said Jerry jocularly.

"Now, now. Don't get too cheeky," responded Cuthbert.

Everyone laughed at the playful banter between the two.

"Message from Commodore Harewood, sir," one of the ratings said as he handed a scribbled piece of paper to the captain. "I just decoded it."

"Ah. Thank you, Johnston," the captain replied, taking the piece of paper and reading the message. "He says, 'All the best on your trip to the sunshine island. Don't allow the *Tuna* to get caught whilst you have small fish onboard. Good luck to all and God be with you, to my two young friends. P.S. After the war, maybe they will arrange for me to do a summer season of paid singing in their theatre!' "

"Did the Commodore really sing for you?" the captain asked, lifting his cap and wiping his forehead.

"Oh yes, he did. He's a great singer," Linda replied.

"I'll say he is. Even the vice admiral has asked him to sing just for him. I'm told that whilst he's based in Scotland he's learning to play the bagpipes."

"Oh, he certainly knows one Scottish song anyway," Brian replied, "because he sang one to us when we arrived in Kylesku, but he didn't play the bagpipes."

The journey down through the Irish Sea was long and rather boring. It was not at all like the trip they had taken north when they had stood on the deck of *La Capricieuse* and admired the stunning scenery and mountains of the Western Isles. Occasionally Captain Lewis allowed them to climb to the top of the conning tower to look out. However, most of the time was spent inside the increasingly stuffy atmosphere of the submarine. Here they whiled away the time playing charades and card games whilst the submarine made slow but steady progress. It took over a day and a half before they finally passed the Bishop Rock Lighthouse on the Scilly Isles and broke out into the English Channel.

"Be on high alert," the captain called over the loudspeaker system as his voice echoed throughout the submarine. "We are coming into the Channel, so keep your eyes and ears open for enemy activity."

As they left the relative safety of the Irish Sea, Jerry, Linda, Cuthbert and Brian detected that everyone was becoming a little more tense.

"It would have been so much easier to have transported you to Guernsey," the captain commented as he studied some charts laid out on a table in front of him. "It lies further out in the Channel where the water is deeper, whereas Jersey is sheltered by the Cherbourg Peninsula and then Normandy. We will have to steer between Alderney and Guernsey and then get as close to the north coast of Jersey as possible, all without alerting the Germans that we are in the vicinity," he explained as he ran his fingers over the charts to show his dilemma. "We then have to launch the dingy with you two on board and several of my men in order to row you ashore. It's some operation that has landed on my plate."

He pressed a button and spoke into the loudspeaker system. "This is the captain speaking. We will be going in to drop off Jack and Jill at zero plus one hours. We are now going to action stations. Landing crew, do your final checks and prepare for departure. I wish you all good luck."

"I think we'll need a lot of luck to pull this off," Brian commented seriously.

"I think it's prayer we need more than luck, Brian," Linda replied.

"Yes, Linda, I think you are right," Brian said with a smile.

"Crash dive, crash dive!" someone shouted, bringing their conversation to an abrupt end. "Crash dive," the captain repeated over the loudspeaker before adding, "Enemy ship approaching. Maintain silent routine!"

Suddenly, Jerry and Linda noticed that for the first time the familiar vibration and humming of the engines had stopped and that everything and everyone was very silent. As they looked around, they also noticed that every one of the submariners' faces was looking up. Then they heard a faint droning noise that seemed to become progressively louder.

"Engines," the captain whispered. "They are right above us."

Another minute of tense silence passed before a tremendous muffled explosion rocked the submarine, caused the lights to flicker and sent Jerry flying into some pipes across from where he had been standing.

"What was that?" Cuthbert whispered in alarm.

"Depth charges," Captain Lewis replied as he gave orders to flood another tank in order to take *Tuna* to a deeper depth.

Another muffled explosion sent further shockwaves through the submarine. This time everyone was already hanging on tightly to anything solid that was close to hand.

"The German ship is moving away," the captain said as he looked from the control room above his head toward the hatch that led to the conning tower. "Thankfully, although they must have seen us, they did not get an accurate fix on us so they were just scattering depth charges in a random pattern in the hope of hitting us."

"What are depth charges?" Linda asked.

"Big bombs fired from a ship that sink and explode next to submarines," Jerry quickly replied before the captain had a chance to answer.

"Well, yes, sort of. They are canisters filled with explosives along with a hydrostatic fuse that can be set to explode at different depths. Thankfully, the water around us acts as a cushion and absorbs a lot of the power, but if one gets close enough it could easily sink the submarine and all of us with it," the captain added.

"A very cheery thought," Cuthbert added grimly as he held tightly to some pipes for dear life.

"Captain," a voice spoke in a loud whisper from the far side of the room. "Sonar has picked up propellers coming in on our starboard beam."

"Hold on, everyone," Captain Lewis spoke as loudly as he dared. "They are continuing to attack."

Everyone took a fresh grip of anything immovable as the distant, steady hum of the enemy ship sounded somewhere above them.

"BOOM!" Another great explosion sent the submarine rocking from side to side.

"Flood all tanks," the captain ordered the young man who was next to a screen with some gauges opposite him. "We'll sit tight on the bottom."

"I'm afraid we can't, sir," interrupted another man who was sitting at a small table upon which were several books of charts. "The bottom is way too deep here. We are around

Hurd's Deep, which is nearly six hundred feet deep, twice our safe maximum depth."

Captain Lewis let out a sigh as another distant explosion sounded throughout the submarine. "Okay, take her down to maximum depth, three hundred feet, and hold her steady," he commanded.

"Group down, steady as she goes," someone echoed.

More distant rumbles could be heard as the attacking German ship moved away into the distance and everyone on board felt the submarine drop once more through the cold, grey water of the English Channel.

"Three hundred feet, sir," said the man with the charts while tapping a gauge in front of him.

"Okay, hold her steady here," the captain again commanded.

"Could I make a suggestion, sir?" one of the other officers said as he looked at a piece of paper that he had been scribbling on.

"Yes, of course. What's on your mind?" Captain Lewis replied.

"Propellers again," another man said.

"Prepare for another attack," the captain said. "Pass the word along."

"Just an idea, sir," said the young officer with the piece of paper, "but I've noticed, from tracking the enemy by sonar, that twice now when that ship has attacked it has passed over us, run on for about half a mile, turned to port to run in and then attacked us again."

"Well?"

"Well, it seems to be coming back and attacking again. If it then turns to port after it has passed above us, we could be ready to attack whilst she is on the turn. Then she will show us a nice juicy broadside, just ideal for a salvo of torpedoes."

"Yes, but we'd have to start our engine to rise close to the surface and that would give the game away as to where we are," Captain Lewis answered as he studied the piece of paper his colleague was holding.

"Isn't it worth a try?" the officer said. "If it works, we sink it, if not, we crash dive and hope for the best."

Another distant rumble growled as more depth charges were fired quite a distance away. Captain Lewis looked at Jerry and Linda, who like everyone else were holding on tightly. He raised his cap and scratched his head. "Okay. Load number one and number two torpedo tubes. Prepare to attack!"

CHAPTER 25

"I really don't like this idea at all," Cuthbert finally said, easing his grip slightly on the pipes that his arms were tightly clamped around.

"I'm too keen on those navigation officers' thoughts of just hoping for the best if we miss," Brian added. "It seems to me that, at the moment, that German ship is just guessing at where we are, but if we miss with our torpedoes, it will know exactly where we are."

"Then let's pray that we don't miss," Jerry suggested.

"Yes, let's do that," Linda agreed. "We do need to trust in more than luck. I read just yesterday, in Uncle Fred's Bible, two verses that seem to say the same thing. Here," she motioned to Jerry, "would you mind passing me the Bible, please?"

Jerry reached into the bag for the Bible. Linda took the tatty-looking, black leather book and began to flick through its pages.

"Here they are, in the book called Psalms," she said excitedly. "Psalm forty-two, verses five and eleven. 'Why art thou cast down, O my soul? And why art thou disquieted in me? Hope thou in God.' That's the secret," she added as another distant explosion shook the submarine. "We need to hope in God. Only He can help us."

"Full ahead group up," Captain Lewis barked over the loudspeaker. "Prepare to attack."

The submarine rose at a rapid angle and at an alarming rate as its engines whined to bring it from its hiding place in the deep to a position in which it could attack the enemy ship.

"Periscope depth," the captain called as he raised the large cylindrical tube in the centre of the control room. "Prepare number one and number two forward tubes."

The captain turned his cap back to front and looked into the binocular-like contraption that allowed him to see above the surface of the water.

"Periscope depth," someone said.

The captain swung the periscope round until he could see the enemy ship.

"We are in position," one of the officers said.

"Right, let's just hope he turns again to port. If he does, we fire two as he turns and another two immediately after. Understand?"

"Yes, sir," came the reply.

"Turn, turn, turn," Captain Lewis whispered under his breath. "Looks like it is continuing on a straight course."

"But if it had sonar it must have heard us start up the motors," the navigation officer answered.

"Maybe it didn't have sonar and that's why its depth charges were so off target," the captain replied. "It was probably just going by a brief visual sighting of us. No, wait. Yes, it is turning! Fire number one and number two torpedoes."

There was a moment of calm before the submarine shuddered as two torpedoes left its front tubes, heading in the direction of the enemy ship.

"Prepare for second attack," Captain Lewis barked. "Ready, ready, fire!"

Another vibration shook the submarine as another two torpedoes went on their way towards the German ship.

Captain Lewis kept his face pressed hard into the periscope as the German ship continued its turn to port, unaware of the great danger that was rapidly coming closer. Suddenly, there was an explosion far louder than any they had heard previously and whoops of delight rang out from all the sailors throughout the *Tuna*.

"Direct hit," Captain Lewis said, still staring through his periscope.

Then another loud explosion roared as a second torpedo rammed into the side of the German vessel.

"Right on," Captain Lewis said. "Good shooting.

Congratulations all round. All right, the Germans know we are here now, so we had better head back home. No point risking anything else. Give me a heading to Portsmouth."

"But what about Jersey?" Jerry asked desperately.

"Oh, I'm sorry," Captain Lewis said, "but it's just too dangerous now. That ship will have let others know that we are around so we need to get away. We can't afford to head further into enemy waters. Don't worry, we'll try again. Unfortunately it just won't be tonight. Do you want to take a peek at the ship we just hit?"

Despite Jerry's great disappointment, he took the periscope and looked through, staring in disbelief at the burning wreck he could see before him. He watched by the light of the fire as men threw themselves off the ship's blazing decks into the sea, then, just as some appeared to be launching some kind of lifeboat, another massive explosion lit up the night sky and the ship was gone. As Jerry turned away, he said, "Those poor, poor men."

"They were Germans!" a naval rating said from behind him. "It was either them or us. They deserved to die, every one of them."

"No, they didn't," Jerry replied firmly as he wiped tears from his eyes. "They didn't deserve to die. They were just carrying out their orders, just as you were. They were human beings."

"Oh, you're just a lad," another sailor sniggered. "What do you know about war?"

"Jerry was in St. Helier when the German air force bombed us," Linda replied, cutting across the sailors' comments. "He knows about war. We had people killed in Jersey that day. They were good men going about their business, but they were killed. We know what the Germans can do but we also know that not all of them are bad. There were some good, kind Germans in Jersey who didn't want the war any more than we did." She stopped when she realised that just about everyone had ceased their merriment to listen to her.

"Linda's right," Jerry added. "They are not all bad!"

"Well, they are all rotten to the core to me," someone else added. "I lost a set of grandparents last year in the blitz on London. They were good people too, just blown to bits when a bomb landed on their house."

"All right, all right. Enough," Captain Lewis intervened. "It's bad enough having to fight the Germans, never mind fallings out inside a submarine under my command. Now, back to your stations, all of you."

"But what about survivors?" Linda enquired. "Are you not going to see if you can rescue any of those men from that ship?"

"It would be too dangerous. If other enemy ships came or a U-boat appeared we could end up in the same situation as them," the captain replied sadly.

"Those men, though," Jerry added in bewilderment, "that I saw jumping into the sea, they will all drown unless we help them."

"I would think that most are already dead, especially if they didn't have lifejackets. The water is so cold I doubt there will be any survivors."

"But what if there are?" Linda added. "There must be some we can save."

Cuthbert smiled at the captain, seeing his dilemma. "I told you before, they are only young, but by gum they don't half know how to argue their case!"

Captain Lewis hesitated before bending down to the loudspeaker. "Prepare to surface and pick up survivors," he ordered, "but keep a close look out for enemy activity."

"Thank you," Linda said quietly as she silently prayed that nothing would happen to them as they tried to pick up survivors.

Once Captain Lewis had brought *Tuna* to the surface, several men exited through one of the hatches to stand on the deck to see if there were going to be any survivors.

"Up top," the captain commanded Jerry and Linda. "It was your idea, so I guess that any survivors we pick up will wish to thank you two."

As they climbed on to the deck they could hear distant voices calling in desperation, "Hilf mir! Hilf mir!"

"What are they saying?" Jerry asked one of the sailors.

"Help me," Linda answered without hesitation.

"How do you know that?" Jerry asked in astonishment.

"Have you forgotten already, Jerry, that I learnt some German before we left Jersey so that I could try to listen in on German conversations in case they were saying anything important."

"Oh, yes, I'd clean forgotten," Jerry replied in a chastened manner.

"Can't we get closer to them?" Linda shouted from the deck to Captain Lewis, who was now standing on top of the conning tower directing a handheld searchlight towards the sound of the voices.

"We have to go slowly so we don't run anyone over," he replied, "and we need to give them time to get to us so we can haul them aboard." As he spoke, his searchlight picked out through the darkness the form of a man struggling in the water.

"Hilf...mir...Hilf...mir," the man spluttered as he fought to stay afloat.

The captain carefully steered the submarine slowly towards the struggling German sailor, and as he drew alongside, several hands reached down to help pull him out of the water and onto the deck of the submarine.

"Oh...Danke sehr, danke sehr," the man stammered, shivering with cold.

Slowly the large submarine drew closer to where other voices could be heard calling for help. It seemed to both Jerry and Linda that the sounds were growing more distant, even though they were moving closer to them.

"Why are they swimming away from us when we are trying to help?" Jerry called up to the captain.

"They aren't swimming away from us. They are dying from hypothermia in the water," Captain Lewis replied, "and possibly from injuries as well. Unfortunately, that's the consequence of war."

"There's another," Jerry called as through the gloom he saw a head bobbing in the water a few yards away.

Slowly the submarine pulled alongside the almost motionless figure being kept afloat by his lifejacket.

As hands reached down to pull him up, one of the sailors said, "He's dead. Leave him be."

"Are you sure?" another asked.

"Yes, quite sure. He's dead."

"Okay, put him back in the water," another commanded.

Jerry and Linda stared in disbelief at the body of the young German sailor as he was carefully dropped back into the sea. He looked so young. In fact, not much older than they were themselves and now he was dead, his body being left alone and forsaken in the cold, dark waters of the English Channel.

"I wonder who his parents are?" Linda asked as she watched the lifeless body disappear into the darkness.

Jerry watched him disappear too. "That's the first time I have ever seen a dead body. He looked so white and frightened."

"Over there," the captain shouted as he swung his searchlight round to where another faint call could be heard. The penetrating beam picked out the silhouette of two more sailors, one trying to keep the other afloat and swim towards the submarine. It was a pathetic sight as neither seemed to have the strength or ability to swim any closer to the help that was awaiting them. "Two degrees to starboard," Captain Lewis ordered. "Steady, steady, stop engines."

Once again, hands reached down from the deck of the submarine towards the two men. As they were pulling the second man aboard, one of the British sailors recoiled in shock. "Ugh. He's got no legs!" he exclaimed.

"And he's dead," another responded as he looked down on the motionless figure.

"Bitte speichern Sie ihn, er ist mein Freund!" his colleague called out, then pausing, he added in English, "Please!"

"What's he saying, Linda?" Jerry enquired.

"I'm not too sure, but I think it's something to do with being friends," Linda answered as she knelt next to the first man.

He looked up with startled eyes and stared into her pretty face. Then he looked around at the sailors who had pulled him on board, before looking back towards Linda. It was clear that he was shocked to see not just a woman, but a young teenager, kneeling next to him on the deck of a British submarine.

"Wer bist du?" he asked.

"What's he saying?" Jerry asked again.

"He wants to know who I am, I think," she replied.

"Mein Name ist Linda," Linda replied.

The motionless man lying at his side gave a moan, and Brian, who was now on deck, went to his aid. It was all too obvious that he was very seriously injured. "We need to get this man below decks," Brian said to a couple of sailors who were looking on, "but be careful. He's already in a lot of pain and also in shock."

"We need to dive," Captain Lewis shouted from his elevated position. "Everyone below. We have picked up sounds of approaching shipping on the sonar. We are making for Portsmouth."

CHAPTER 26

Blankets were passed to the two uninjured survivors, whilst Brian got out his medic's bag and started working on the man with no legs.

"How is he?" Captain Lewis asked as he squatted down next to Brian.

"Worst injuries I've ever had to deal with," Brian replied dryly. "They never teach you how to deal with things like this in nursing school. Both legs blown clean off just above the knee. I'm surprised the shock hasn't killed him, never mind the loss of blood. Then again, I think that the water might well have saved him, being so cold. It would have constricted the blood flow a bit. How long before we reach land and proper medical help?"

"About eight hours steaming at full speed on the surface," the captain replied. "Can he last that long?"

"I'll be able to answer that when we get there," Brian replied as he used his scissors to cut another piece of loose flesh from the stump of one of the man's upper legs. "If we keep him warm and sedated with plenty of chloroform he might just make it. Anyway, I'll do my best for him. It's a strange thing," he continued as he sought to clean up the remains of the sailor's other leg, "but this is the first German I have seen, in real life, I mean. I thought I'd be trying to kill them and here I am trying to save his life!"

Linda and Jerry were sitting with the injured sailor's friend as Linda tried in her limited German to find out more about him.

Suddenly a young officer appeared. "The captain has sent me to help you," he said as he sat down opposite the two German sailors who were still shivering, but drinking hot coffee. "I'm Sub-Lieutenant Andy Root and I can speak fluent German."

"Oh, great," Linda replied, fidgeting nervously. "I've been trying but I only have a few phrases and I can't understand what they are saying."

The sub-lieutenant smiled, and turning to the German sailors, spoke to them in their own language. After receiving the reply, he turned to Jerry and Linda. "He says you sank his ship but saved his life and he thanks you from the bottom of his heart."

"Please tell him it was all of us who saved his life," Linda replied and then listened to the two-way conversation, this time with the other sailor also chipping in.

"They both say that this pretty young woman saved their lives and they thank you," he translated as Linda blushed with embarrassment.

"Well, I like that! I never got a mention," Jerry said cheekily.

There was a further conversation between Andy and the two Germans before Andy again turned to the two youngsters. "They want to know why you are on this submarine."

"Yes, I guess they are wondering about that," Cuthbert responded as he walked up to the group. "It's something I too have been thinking about a lot as well. Why am I here on a submarine in the English Channel?"

"You're here to help us get back home and today you were here to help rescue these German sailors," Jerry reminded him.

"Tell the men that we are from Jersey," Linda said, looking at Andy.

"Diese jungen Menschen sind von Jersey und versuchen wieder in ihre Häuser dort," the sub-lieutenant translated.

As soon as the German who had kept his injured friend afloat heard the name of Jersey, his face lit up with obvious excitement and pleasure and he began to jabber away, twenty to the dozen, in his own language.

"What's he saying?" Jerry asked.

"I'm not sure. He was speaking so fast," the sub-lieutenant answered. "Something about having a relative in Jersey."

"Well, I don't think there were any German people living on the Island before the army invaded," Linda said, frowning a little.

"No, but maybe he has a relative stationed there now with the army," Jerry suggested as he looked at the two shivering sailors.

"I'll try again," Andy said, turning back to the two men.

After much conversation between the Germans and the submariner, Sub-Lieutenant Andy eventually turned back to Jerry and Linda.

"This man has an older cousin stationed in the army on Jersey," he explained. "He says he likes Jersey but does not like being in Hitler's army, taking away people's freedom."

"Tell him we were trying to get back to Jersey and to our families and that my parents are being held in prison in Jersey along with a man called Pierre Le Blanc," Linda replied.

More conversation followed which Linda tried hard to understand, but eventually gave up as it was too rapid.

"He thinks we are trying to put marines ashore on Jersey because your friend there was in an army uniform," Andy said, turning towards Linda and Jerry.

"Oh," Linda retorted in surprise. "Please tell him that Cuthbert and Brian are our friends and are here just to look after us and help us get back home to Jersey so that the Germans will release my parents from prison."

As the message was relayed, the German's face beamed. He spoke very quickly to Andy but looked at Linda.

"He says his cousin will get you back home if he could ask him. He says he's an officer, an Oberleutnant in the occupation force. He also says that because you, Fräulein, saved his life, he wants to help you get back home."

"What is an Oberleutnant?" Jerry asked.

Another question was asked in German and the sailor gave his reply, gesticulating with his hands.

"Apparently it's some rank above a captain, so he might

have a bit of clout to help you two get back home," Andy answered with a smile.

A look of intense pain passed across the German sailor's face as he spoke again to Andy, motioning with his hands. Even Jerry and Linda could see that he was asking about his injured shipmate.

Eight hours later, the *Tuna* sailed into Portsmouth Harbour. Miraculously, the injured sailor was still alive, thanks in no small part to Brian, who had not only bandaged his severe wounds to protect them and stop the bleeding, but had never left his side the whole time.

Once the submarine was safely berthed, Jerry and Linda looked on as the injured man was very carefully extricated from the cramped confines of HMS *Tuna*, and his two fellow sailors were helped off the boat.

"Do you really think that man's cousin could help us get back to Jersey?" Linda asked Captain Lewis as they walked slowly along the jetty towards some large red brick buildings in the distance.

"I'm not sure, because as a prisoner of war he will not be allowed to make contact with anyone on the German side. We will notify his immediate relatives through the Red Cross of his position as our prisoner. However, that is usually as far as any contact goes," the captain explained as he watched a look of great disappointment cross both Jerry's and Linda's faces.

"Oh," Linda sighed, "I really thought that he might be the key to us getting home."

"I am sorry that our mission last night failed, especially when we had made such good progress. We will hopefully receive further orders to try again tomorrow but it will be a full moon, so much more dangerous and the Germans patrolling around the Channel Islands may well be on high alert after last night." He paused. "I'm not too sure whether the War Office will allow you two to be put at so much risk."

"So do you mean you will not be trying to take us again?" Jerry asked anxiously.

Linda was numb. She felt all hope of getting her parents out of danger had gone.

Jerry looked at her and simply said, "God has to have a reason."

She still felt sick to the pit of her stomach, but the tears wouldn't come.

"Why don't we get something to eat?" suggested Cuthbert.

Linda nodded, unable to think clearly. She doubted she could eat anything, but followed anyway.

They had some lunch and Jerry tried with his usual cheek to make a few jokes, but he failed in any attempt to cheer anyone up.

After a fretful sleep in a quickly arranged boarding house and a tasteless breakfast the next morning, eaten mostly in silence, Brian spoke up. "Anyone want to join me in a trip to the hospital to see how my friend Othman is getting on?"

Linda's face lit up.

"Othman?" Cuthbert questioned. "Is that the name of the sailor who lost both his legs?"

"Yes, it is," Brian answered. "He's twenty-eight and married with two children, one four and the other a baby. He lived in the Saarland."

"You learned a lot about him during our trip to Portsmouth," Jerry said.

"Well, I was trying to keep him talking and occupied because I felt if he slipped into unconsciousness he might never wake up. The sub-lieutenant chap, Andy, was a real help because he speaks fluent German. Anyway, Othman wanted to talk about his family once we had got his wet clothes off him and wrapped him in dry blankets. He was jabbering away about his wife and children so I just questioned him about them," Brian explained. "I would think that he'll be unconscious for most of today because they will have had to try and tidy up what's left of his legs."

"I would really like to see him," Linda spoke a little more brightly, although she still looked downcast.

Brian looked across at her. "Don't give up, Linda. There may be a way."

"I don't think so," she replied. "We only have two days until the twentieth, but as Jerry said, God will have a reason." She turned away as she felt the tears coming and braced herself for the visit to see Othman.

"I just feel so sorry for that young man who we tried to save last night," Jerry suddenly added. "He looked so young and there we were, ready to help him, but he'd already died. He was so near to being saved."

"Hello," Cuthbert said. "I feel another of your sermons coming on about being so close to becoming a Christian, but lost."

"I hadn't even thought about it," Linda smiled weakly, "but I guess there is some truth in it. Just imagine hearing about what the Lord Jesus has done for you on the cross and never trusting Him and missing out on heaven forever. It would be awful!"

"I knew it," Cuthbert answered. "Come on, let's head off to the hospital before we get a full sermon!"

CHAPTER 27

That night, the four friends returned from the hospital, having been told that Othman was doing well despite his injuries. They found that Captain Lewis had arrived to join them for dinner.

"I have some interesting information to pass on," he said conspiratorially as he leaned over his plate towards the centre of the table. "When I reported today at my debrief about Andy Root and his conversation with Erich Werner, one of the two uninjured sailors, there was quite a kerfuffle. Phone calls were made to London and the upshot is that someone in London is going to try and get in touch with a contact in Jersey. In turn, it is hoped that they will be able to contact Erich's cousin, a certain Oberleutnant Anton Scholz, who is stationed there. With some diplomacy and the willing help of Erich, it is hoped that some strings can be pulled in the German army."

Cuthbert shook his head in disbelief. "This is just incredible!"

"But what if his cousin won't help?" Brian asked. "And even if he does help, how do we get Jerry and Linda to him?"

"I don't know. That still has to be arranged. However, I don't think it will be by submarine," the captain said, grinning broadly, "for which I take it you will all be pretty glad."

"Isn't time running out for them, Captain?" Brian asked, not wanting to get Linda's hopes up for them to be dashed again.

"We know that," Captain Lewis replied. "Everything is being done as quickly as possible. If this doesn't work, then..." He turned away. There wasn't really another plan.

Cuthbert chipped in quickly, "I think it will work."

"You will be coming with us, won't you?" Linda enquired,

looking at Cuthbert and Brian as they continued eating. "I mean, if this works out. You can't just abandon us now, can you?"

"I think," Brian added, piercing a carrot with his fork and waving it towards the two young friends, "we have been in this from the start and we will still be there at the end. We will be going with you whether Captain Lewis lets us or not."

"That's a relief," Jerry said. "I mean, we have been through a lot together in these last two months and it wouldn't seem right to just leave for home without you two still being with us."

"Well, I sure do appreciate the vote of confidence in us," Cuthbert added. "I would definitely prefer not to go back in one of those cramped, smelly tin cans that the navy calls a submarine!"

"Well," said Captain Lewis, pleased to leave his charges in a more positive frame of mind, but still concerned as to exactly what the outcome of this new suggestion would be. "We will know more sometime tomorrow, so it's a case of sitting tight and waiting, I'm afraid." The captain placed his knife and fork together on his empty plate. "Anyway, I have to go back to my office, but I'll be in touch with you once again tomorrow. Goodnight, all."

The next day, the late September sun had risen high and bright in the sky by the time that Jerry and Linda appeared in the little dining room. Exhausted from their submarine adventure, they had slept beyond their agreed getting up time of 8:00 a.m.

"Ah, here at last," Brian teased as they came through the doorway. "We were starting to think that maybe you had left us during the night and decided to swim back home."

"Ha-ha! Very funny," they both laughed as they took their seats at the breakfast table. Brian and Cuthbert were relieved that Jerry and Linda seemed to have their sense of humour back.

"Have we heard any news yet?" Linda enquired eagerly.

"It's only half past nine. The navy won't have got out of their hammocks yet," Cuthbert answered, trying to keep everybody cheerful with his usual humorous spirit.

"No, of course we won't have done," a voice answered from the doorway behind Cuthbert's chair. "Probably because, unlike you lot, us sailor boys never managed to get into our bunks last night!" It was Captain Lewis, who was walking across to the table where the four were seated. He gave Cuthbert a hearty slap on the back.

"Oh, well, er, um, I didn't mean it like that," Cuthbert stammered in surprise.

"I know, I know," the captain replied with humour. "If I'd have been in your shoes, I would have said just the same about the army."

"Is there any news yet about us going back to Jersey?" Linda asked, anxiety showing in her eyes.

"We are still working on it, but it seems that Erich's offer was genuine. We now have to get our contact in Jersey to get in touch with Anton Scholz, who has to agree to help us out," Captain Lewis explained. "It takes time to get all these things to fall into place."

"Oh dear," Linda replied, a sense of panic in her voice again, "and here I was thinking that we would be on our way this afternoon."

The captain looked compassionately at Linda and said, "As soon as we get some news, I will be in touch. I also came to tell you that Othman has been asking for you all. Apparently when he came round, all he could say was 'Brian'. Then he was asking to see all his rescuers. I assume he means you two, Jerry and Linda. I'm sure you'll have a good time visiting him because if it wasn't for you he wouldn't be here."

Linda looked at Jerry. "Maybe God has a different purpose in all this. I'm just going to have to be patient and trust in Him."

The four arrived at the hospital around lunchtime and were ushered into the ward where the injured German sailor was being treated. Standing outside the little room in which

Othman was lying was a soldier with his gun slung across his shoulder.

When he saw the sergeant's stripes on Cuthbert's uniform, he pulled himself up quickly, standing to attention and saluting smartly.

"At ease," Cuthbert said. "Can we visit the prisoner, please?"

"Yes, sir," the soldier replied, opening the door.

As they walked in, Othman stirred in his bed and turned to look at them. As soon as he saw Linda and Jerry behind the sergeant, his face beamed with an enormous smile. "I...thank...you!" Then he caught sight of Brian entering the room and repeated the phrase once again to him. "I...thank... you!"

Linda went up to Othman's bed and smiled down at him. "Hallo," she said in his own language. "Mein Name ist Linda."

"Even I can make that one out," Cuthbert, whose German was non-existent, chuckled. "She's telling him her name."

Once again, Othman's face lit up as he heard Linda speaking in his own native tongue. "Mein Name ist Othman," he replied happily.

Linda paused, trying hard to remember the right words to use as a reply. "Ja...ich...weiß..." she stammered, "wie geht es dir?"

"What did she say?" Brian enquired.

"He was telling me his name," Linda translated, "and I told him that I already knew his name but wanted to know how he was. At least, that is what I was trying to say."

"Hello. Who have we here?" a tall, balding man, dressed in a long white coat and wearing a pair of round rimmed spectacles, asked as he entered the room.

"Oh, hello, Doctor," said Brian as he turned to face him.

"Are you the good folks that Othman keeps telling me saved his life?" the doctor asked as he looked at some notes at the side of his patient's bed. "I'm Doctor Thomas, by the way."

"Well, I'm not sure you could really accuse us of saving his life," Brian added, "but we did the best we could for him given the circumstances."

The doctor turned to Othman and spoke to him in German and then listened to the reply.

"He's adamant that he owes his life to you two young people and Brian who tended to him in the submarine," the doctor said as he looked up from Othman.

"Well, we only did what any human being would be prepared to do for another," Brian answered truthfully.

Othman mumbled something and tried to reach across to a small cabinet next to his bed, but stopped short with a groan of pain. He then spoke to the doctor in German.

"He wants me to get something out of his bedside cabinet," the doctor said as he opened a door and pulled out a small black wallet that was still damp.

Othman reached out to take it, and opening it up, carefully pulled out something that had once been a photograph but was now totally unrecognisable as such. He looked at the ruined image in total astonishment and big tears started to well up in his eyes and roll down his cheeks as he spoke sadly to the doctor.

"He says this was a photograph of his wife that he always kept with him and that it has been ruined in the water. He will never be able to look and see how lovely she is."

Othman quickly looked through the other small flaps in the wallet and eventually pulled out what was obviously another small photo. This time his face became radiant as he turned the image towards his watching visitors, saying simply, "Meine Kinder."

"Oh, bless him," Linda said, tears filling her eyes as well. "The poor man has lost his wife's photo but has still got the one of his children."

Othman clutched the precious photo to his chest, along with the now ruined one of his wife, and wept.

The doctor spoke to him in German, and Othman's face changed as he listened and then replied again.

"I told him that I would dry his wallet out along with the picture of his children," the doctor explained, "then Othman said that he had lost his legs, his freedom, the picture of his wife and the joy of his children all because of Adolf Hitler."

"Wow," Cuthbert said in surprise. "That's a bit dramatic! Someone fighting in the German navy doesn't like old Adolf."

The doctor spoke once again to the German sailor who beckoned for Linda and Jerry to come closer to his bed. As they approached, he spoke to the doctor, who translated. "He says that he hopes his children will grow up to be just as good and kind as you."

CHAPTER 28

By dinnertime, Jerry and Linda were starting to become despondent at the lack of news from Captain Lewis when they heard the phone ringing in the guesthouse where they were staying.

"Jerry Le Godel," the owner called through the dining room door. She was a rather plump lady with a pale face and unnaturally black hair. "Phone for you."

Jerry got up quickly from the table and made his way into the hallway. The others listened to what they could hear of his end of the conversation.

"Yes, fine, thank you...Any news from Erich or Anton?... Great!...Oh!...Well, yes, I guess so...Thank you!"

"That was short," remarked Brian as Jerry re-entered the room.

"Was it Captain Lewis?" Linda asked eagerly. "And was it good news?"

"Yes, it was Captain Lewis and I guess it was good news because Erich Werner can help us. Things have to be sorted in London, but they have got through a lot of red tape and are now trying to contact his cousin in Jersey to see if he can arrange anything for us. Unfortunately, we just have to sit tight and wait." Jerry paused, then rummaged in his pocket and pulled out a crumpled piece of paper. "I was looking through Uncle Fred's Bible this morning and I read some words about patience. I wrote them down." He cleared his throat. "Here they are. 'Wait on the Lord: be of good courage, and He shall strengthen thine heart: wait, I say, on the Lord.' It's found in Psalm twenty-seven."

"Did you really read that this morning in that Bible?" Brian questioned, looking at Jerry suspiciously.

"It seems to me," Cuthbert replied thoughtfully, "that whenever you two have had a problem or difficulty, you have found some verse or other in the Bible that has been spot on."

"Well, what is surprising about that?" Jerry replied. "If the Bible really is God's Word, then I'd expect Him to speak to me from it just when I need Him to tell me what to do."

"You can't really argue with that, can you?" Cuthbert answered. "Even a great sinner like me can see that logic."

"Yes," Brian responded, a faraway look upon his face. "If there is a God, then I suppose He can meet all our needs if we trust Him. This book has really changed their lives, Cuthbert, and I'm wondering if I need it to change mine."

"It's believing on the Lord Jesus, who died on the cross because of our sins, that will change your life," Jerry answered.

"It was when we trusted Him as our Saviour that we discovered that the Bible can guide us every day if we really let it," Linda added.

"You know, when we were in the *Tuna* the other night and being depth charged I was terrified of two things," Brian explained. "One was dying and the other was dying underwater. I've been wondering why I am scared to die if death is the end and there is nothing after death. I think that I am really scared to die because, deep down, right from Sunday school days, I have known that there is a God and maybe I will have to meet Him someday. If what I learned at Sunday school is right and if what I have seen and heard Jerry and Linda doing and saying is also right, then I too need to be saved."

"Oh," was all that Cuthbert could manage after listening to his friend's reasoning.

"Do you really mean that?" Linda questioned earnestly.

"Yes, I do," Brian replied in a shaky voice. "I put it off back when I was younger but I think that, through you, God is giving me a second chance to get right with Him. I really need to take it now and not put it off as I did before."

"Then don't wait," Jerry encouraged. "It changed my Uncle Fred's life and it changed Linda's and my life and I'm sure that it will do the same for you too, Brian."

"If you don't mind, I'd like to be excused and go to my room as I think I need to be alone with God for a few minutes." Brian rose to leave the table. "I need to get it sorted and settled once and for all tonight."

It was half an hour before Brian reappeared, but when he did so, Jerry, Linda and Cuthbert knew that something big had taken place in his life. "You know, I will never forget this little guesthouse here in the Copnor area of Portsmouth and that little bedroom upstairs. I'll never forget you two, Linda and Jerry, and I will never forget tonight because I have just trusted the Lord Jesus as my Saviour and am now on the road to heaven."

"That's great, Brian," Jerry and Linda seemed to say together.

"That's the best news that we have heard since arriving from Jersey in July," Jerry continued. "That means there are three of us all saved and ready for heaven. How wonderful!"

Cuthbert said nothing. He looked uncomfortable.

"Oh, Cuthbert, what about you?" Linda looked at him kindly.

Cuthbert was clearly at a loss as to what to say. "I really thought everyone was going to heaven."

"Even Adolf Hitler?" Brian questioned.

"Oh, well, no, not him, or Joseph Goebbels or Heinrich Himmler or any of those crazy Nazis," Cuthbert countered. "No, just all good people. Look, let's leave this discussion until another day when my thinking might be straighter."

As Cuthbert made his way to his room for the night, followed by Linda and Jerry, Brian said, "Now that I am a Christian, I shall join you two in praying for my best buddy, Cuthbert."

As the morning of the nineteenth dawned, Jerry and Linda were anxious to hear of further plans to return them to Jersey. The pressure of time running out made Linda subdued again.

As they finished breakfast, they could hear the phone once again ringing in the hallway. Soon Cuthbert was called to come to the phone. It was a much longer conversation than Jerry had had the previous evening, and despite their best endeavours at listening in to Cuthbert's side, the other three struggled to make head or tale of what was being said. Eventually, after about ten minutes, Cuthbert hung up and returned to their table.

"Well?" Brian questioned eagerly.

"That was Captain Lewis again and the news is good," he responded. "It does seem that all of what Erich has told those questioning him, about his cousin in Jersey, is correct. Apparently Erich was almost brought up by Anton's parents so they are more like brothers than cousins. Erich was sure his cousin would help because apparently he is really appalled at what has gone on in Germany and in the German army the last few years. The Red Cross have been able to make contact with Erich's cousin Anton because he is, in fact, his next of kin. Anton has now made contact with a British informer in Jersey and has agreed to make arrangements to get you two back home safely. According to the informer in Jersey, who must have taken a terrible risk in allowing himself to be made known to a serving German officer, Anton is a perfect gentleman and speaks fluent English. All we have to do is arrange transport for you down the Channel and then put you off in a motor launch. Anton will arrange a place to meet us somewhere off the coast of Jersey whilst we are still out of range of fire from the German army. He will then escort you both to Jersey."

"That's just great," Jerry said, beaming from ear to ear.

"But what about the release of my parents? Will we get there in time?" asked Linda.

"God works in a mysterious way, His wonders to perform," Cuthbert said with an almost innocent look on his face, then added, "We leave late this afternoon."

"Wow and wow," Brian responded. "Where did you learn about God working in mysterious ways?"

"It was part of a hymn that we used to sing in church," Cuthbert replied, "but we never learnt anything from the Bible there. We just had to sit and listen to the vicar reading dull, boring sermons that went on and on and on."

"You never told me before that you went to church," Brian reprimanded.

"It wasn't the happiest experience of my childhood, to be honest. In fact, I made up my mind there and then that if Christianity was as boring as they made it in church, then I wanted nothing more to do with it. I think that is one reason I joined the army, to get a bit of excitement."

"Christianity isn't boring at all," Linda replied. "In fact, becoming a Christian is the best thing that has ever happened to me. You know, I go to bed at night and cannot wait until morning arrives so that I can read Jerry's uncle's Bible to see what God wants to say to me that day. The only disappointment is if I have to wait to read it because Jerry is up first and has started reading it before me." She smiled cheekily.

"Enough of my boring life attending church," Cuthbert announced. "Captain Lewis suggested that we pop in to see Othman again this morning and then head back to Royal Navy headquarters. We may well be leaving later this afternoon so that you can rendezvous with Anton sometime tonight or early tomorrow morning."

"So if everything goes to plan we could be back home by this time tomorrow," Linda suggested confidently.

"Yes," Cuthbert replied. "Come on, let's check out of here and head off to see Othman."

CHAPTER 29

Back at the hospital, Othman beamed as the four walked in to see him for the last time. Linda tried again in her limited German to communicate with him but both she and Othman found the experience rather frustrating until the doctor arrived. Once again, he was able to translate between the injured German sailor and his rescuers.

"He wants to know why you saved anyone from his ship when they had been trying to kill you," the doctor said.

There was a slight embarrassed pause before Jerry spoke up. "A couple of weeks ago, Linda and I learned a very important verse from the Bible at a time when we were being badly bullied by someone. It says, 'Be ye kind one to another, tenderhearted, forgiving one another, even as God for Christ's sake hath forgiven you.' It's in Ephesians chapter four, verse thirty-two. We wanted to save you and the rest of your crew because God had saved us and forgiven us."

The doctor translated. Othman replied, a puzzled look coming across his face as he spoke.

"He wants to know if you believe in God."

"Yes, we do and we believe that His Son, the Lord Jesus, died to take our sins away and make us fit for heaven."

The startled doctor looked at Linda in surprise over the top of his spectacles, then translated to Othman before turning back to them with Othman's reply. "He says that is why you are such a nice person. You are all nice from the inside out."

"I guess that is because God has changed us from the inside out," Jerry answered. Then he looked at the others. "I wonder if somehow we could get Othman a German Bible to read in his own language?"

"That won't be easy," Doctor Thomas commented. "I mean, who wants a German Bible when we are at war with Germany?"

"I'm not sure if Othman wants one or not," Brian commented, "but it really is what he needs to show him the way to heaven."

"Leave it with me," the doctor replied, frowning as if in thought. "I'll see what I can do."

"Promise?" Linda asked.

"Yes, I promise."

Saying goodbye to Othman was not easy. The four felt sorry for him lying there in a foreign hospital, with no legs and a long imprisonment before him. Before they left, Linda promised that once she got back to Jersey she would do her best to arrange to get a replacement photograph of his wife sent to him. How she was going to arrange this, she had no idea, but she knew that somehow God would allow her to perform this small act of kindness.

Captain Lewis was once again on hand to greet them as they arrived back at Portsmouth Harbour. "All set," he said with a smile and jaunty air. He felt that this time things really would work out. "It's all arranged as far as possible," he explained as they walked towards the old red brick building they had first been in before the trip to Scotland. "We leave later this afternoon on *Snowdrop*, and hopefully we will rendezvous with Oberleutnant Anton Scholz somewhere northwest of Jersey."

"Please tell me what *Snowdrop* is," Cuthbert requested as a worried look came over his face.

"HMS *Snowdrop* is one of our Flower-class corvettes," the captain replied amiably. "It's not a submarine like *Tuna*. You'll be okay," he chuckled.

"Whatever is a corvette?" Jerry enquired.

"Oh, sorry, Jerry," Captain Lewis apologised. "A corvette is a small ship. In fact, that is more or less what the name means. *Snowdrop* is a little over nine hundred tons in weight and about two hundred feet long. It was only commissioned at the end of July so it is brand new. It has a top speed of about sixteen knots."

"I have never heard of a corvette before," Jerry replied. "I thought the navy just had destroyers and battleships."

"Oh, Jerry, we need to improve your naval knowledge! We have aircraft carriers, battlecruisers, cruisers, minesweepers and escort ships to name just a few. Every one of them has an important job to do."

Once they were inside the building, the captain pulled a large map out of a drawer and placed it carefully on the table. He ran his hands across the large sheet of paper, flattening the wrinkles. "We leave here at five this evening, steam to this point and hopefully get you off to meet our German 'friend' at around one-thirty tomorrow morning. He should be patrolling this area in a motor launch."

"So we get back just in time. Tomorrow is the twentieth," Linda spoke quietly. She didn't dare to get her hopes high this time, just in case the plan failed again.

The afternoon seemed to drag as they waited to board *Snowdrop*, but they busied themselves watching all the comings and goings of people, ships and vehicles.

"No wonder the Germans keep bombing this place," Brian said to no one in particular. "With all this activity it must be a prime target for the Luftwaffe to try to destroy."

"But isn't it good to know that not all Germans are bad?" Linda said as they watched a canvas-topped lorry rumble past, taking supplies to another ship.

"Well, I was getting rather fond of Othman, and obviously Erich was willing to help us so, no, they can't all be bad," said Jerry, looking at several sailors who were marching smartly in step with an officer at the other side of the berth.

"I think that, with many of the German people, they are sadly caught up in a war they never wanted, and they have no choice but to obey the commands that come from Adolf Hitler," Brian thought aloud. "It's all so terribly sad and tragic to know that many more lives will be lost before the war is over."

At four o'clock, the four boarded *Snowdrop* and began to prepare again for the voyage home.

"I have a friend who has asked if he could accompany us today to ensure that you return in safety," Captain Lewis said as he led them into the ship's mess room.

Jerry breathed out a little sigh of delight and Linda positively beamed with pleasure when they saw Commodore Harewood sitting at a table, reading a large file of papers.

"Hello, again," he said, standing up and moving towards them with his hand outstretched in greeting. "When I heard that our initial attempt to get you home failed, I gained permission from the Admiralty to hotfoot it down here in order to accompany you on this trip. I hope you didn't mind."

"Not at all, sir," Brian said mischievously, "as long as you promise to keep us entertained with some of your songs on the way through the English Channel."

"Oh no, not this time. I'm sorry, but I'm on duty and it wouldn't be right for a commodore to be seen singing and playing the accordion when he has orders to accompany two very important visitors back to their island."

"It's really nice of you to come and see us on our way," Linda said, speaking the words for Jerry too.

"Well then, Captain," the commodore said, "let's get this ship on its way!"

Jerry and Linda were captivated, as they had been on the submarine, by the efficiency of the crew as they all went about their respective jobs before casting off from the quayside. They listened to the dim hum of the ship's diesel motors as they started up and then felt the vibration running through the ship as the two propellers started to turn. They watched as a signalman on the ship's foredeck with a flag in each hand waved them in synchronisation in order to make some sort of signals as the ship slowly moved away from its berth.

"Well, here we go again," said Cuthbert, raising his voice in a spirited fashion. "I only hope we don't see any more action than waving you two off later tonight as you head for home. It really has been delightful knowing you, but it does seem that your thirst for adventure stretches a little further than mine!"

As they pulled out of the inner basin at Portsmouth Harbour, Commodore Harewood took pleasure in pointing out familiar landmarks. "That, on our starboard side, is Gosport and over there, on our port side, is Southsea," he continued, pointing as he commentated, "and that is Hayling Island, over there. In fact, did you know that Portsmouth is an island?"

"Of course it's not," Jerry said with certainty. "An island has to be surrounded by sea, like Jersey and those Scottish islands we saw recently."

"Oh, yes, it is. Most of Portsmouth is situated on Portsea Island. It's cut off from the mainland by a small stretch of water called Portbridge Creek," the commodore explained. "In a minute we will be passing by Bembridge on the Isle of Wight and then Shanklin."

"Shanklin. That's where we stood looking out along the beach and wondering when we'd be going home," Linda recalled. "Who'd ever have thought of us passing by on a British warship, heading out to meet up with a German officer. Things never really work out how you expect, do they?"

"No, I guess not," Commodore Harewood agreed, "and you have certainly had some very interesting and remarkable adventures for two people so young. "

"I'll say we have," Jerry smiled. "You know, I don't think that I will be able to stop talking for a week, telling about all the amazing things I have done and seen."

"Well, Jerry," Commodore Harewood warned, "you are going back to an occupied country, so be careful about how much you say and who you say it to. We have posters up all over the place saying 'Careless talk costs lives'. Just remember that and don't tell anyone about where you went after you arrived on the Isle of Wight. And that goes for you too, Linda. After the war you can tell everyone, but when you both arrive home in the morning just keep silence about some or all of what you did. Can you do that for your king and country, and me as well?"

"That will be hard. I will want to tell my parents so much," Linda replied, "but it will be our secret and yours until the war is over."

"Well done, both of you," the commodore said appreciatively. "I knew I could count on you. Now, let's get you both home!"

CHAPTER 30

Snowdrop sailed steadily along a south-westerly course into the evening. The brightness of the setting sun on the western horizon lit up the sky and the clouds in brilliant colours of orange, red and yellow that made Jerry and Linda stare in awe and wonder at the spectacular display of beauty.

"The sunset always looks good around Corbière, but that is something else tonight," Jerry said.

"You regularly get really stunning sunsets out at sea," the commodore told them.

"Maybe it's a sign from God that everything is going to be all right and this time you will get back home in safety," said Cuthbert as he too admired the sun's rays as it slowly dipped out of sight on the horizon.

"Oh, I hope so," Linda said. "I really do hope so. You have all been so kind to Jerry and me, but I really do want to see my parents again and know that they will not be deported to a prison in Germany."

"We have just received a very important message from the Red Cross in Geneva," Captain Lewis reported as he trotted down a set of metal steps leading from the open bridge of *Snowdrop*. "What do you make of it?" he asked the commodore.

Commodore Harewood read the piece of paper. "Report from German positions in Channel Islands to British Admiralty via Red Cross. All German guns will cease hostilities between midnight and three a.m. to allow safe passage for returning children to the Island of Jersey. During this time, one enemy vessel travelling under the flag of the International Red Cross, and providing the agreed prearranged codes via lamp and Morse signal, will be allowed to enter German territorial waters. Any other allied ships seeking to enter the exclusion zone around the Channel Islands will be considered hostile and will be fired upon without warning. Please acknowledge your intentions to comply with this limited ceasefire via Red Cross Switzerland. Signed Oberst Rudolf Graf von Schmettow."

"I take it that means that the German military authorities in the Channel Islands are providing us with safe passage between midnight and three a.m.," Brian said.

"That's amazing," Cuthbert stated. "No more guns, torpedoes or depth charges."

"Has it been acknowledged by the Admiralty and have we checked that we have the correct codes they have provided?" the commodore enquired of his captain.

"Yes, sir. All done."

"Excellent. Well, it looks like Oberleutnant Anton Scholz has pulled far more strings for us than we could ever have imagined. I mean, that Schmettow chap is the colonel in charge of the Channel Islands. It's pretty much unprecedented for such a thing to happen," Commodore Harewood said, looking thoughtful. "I wonder how he managed it?"

"How can we be sure that we can trust the word of just one German soldier whom none of us have ever met?" Cuthbert enquired as a worried frown spread across his face. "I mean, what if this is all some sort of German trap to sink a British ship?"

"I don't really think that the Germans would go to so much trouble just to sink a nine-hundred-ton corvette," the commodore replied with a smile.

"But aren't you just a tiny bit worried that as soon as we are within range, the German guns will just open up and blow us out of the water?" Cuthbert continued. "It does seem to me that we are trusting totally in the word of just one man. I mean, he might not exist at all."

"Well, we have come this far so we just have to rest on the evidence we have been given and Anton's word through the Red Cross," Commodore Harewood declared. "If the Germans start firing at us when we come closer to the Channel Islands, we will know that his word was not to be trusted."

At midnight, *Snowdrop* flashed her Aldis lamp in the agreed signal pattern as she sailed past Alderney before altering course to south-south-east towards the Island of Jersey. German positions on the island acknowledged her signals as she steamed on her way.

An hour later, *Snowdrop* was approaching its rendezvous point ten miles north of Jersey. As they did so, a distant light from low in the water signalled the presence of another smaller vessel.

"Slow ahead both...Stop engines," they heard Captain Lewis call up on the bridge. Then his voice came over the ship's loudspeaker system. "We are at agreed rendezvous point. Be prepared!"

Commodore Harewood turned to Cuthbert. "Well, Sergeant, it looks like Anton Scholz's word has been absolutely trustworthy even though we have never seen him."

"It's just like being saved, really," Jerry butted in, having overheard both conversations that Commodore Harewood and Cuthbert had held. "I have never seen God, however the evidence of His existence is all around us. Just look at that sunset we witnessed earlier!"

"You never miss an opportunity, do you?" Cuthbert said, smiling. "You know, if I had spent any more time with you two, I might have ended up becoming the Archbishop of Canterbury or something."

"Oh no," Linda laughed. "We'd be happy enough if you just got saved. Anyway, a couple of weeks ago you suggested that I should have that job!"

Out of the darkness, the smaller but very much faster motor launch approached, its signal lamp flashes continuing to be met by those of *Snowdrop*. Eventually it came close enough to see the forms of men standing on its deck. A searchlight flashed from its bows, picking out the Red Cross flag fluttering on the stern of the British corvette.

"We are still observing a ceasefire to allow the safe passage of two children," a voice said in heavily-accented English through a loudhailer. "Will you allow me to come on board and assist in their transfer?"

"Yes, we will," the commodore shouted out through cupped hands. "Pull along our starboard side and we will lower our ladders to you."

The motorboat swung round and pulled along the right hand side of the British ship. It stopped alongside the metal ladders that had been lowered down the side. From the deck of the smaller ship, a man dressed in a smart grey German uniform climbed up and on board *Snowdrop*.

"Good evening," he said. "I am Oberleutnant Anton Scholz." He stood to attention and saluted the commodore and Captain Lewis, who smartly returned his salute.

"Thank you for organising a ceasefire," Commodore Harewood said, offering his right hand in friendship which was warmly taken and pumped vigorously by the German officer. "However did you manage it?"

Anton smiled as he looked around and said simply, "I prayed!"

"You did?" the commodore responded in surprise.

"Yes, I prayed and I told my...how do you say?... commanding officer how my cousin Erich and others had been saved by the two kinder...er, sorry...children. He was not too happy but I told him that we should not be making war on innocent women and children. After a couple of hours my prayers were answered and he agreed to my suggestion."

"Truly astonishing," Captain Lewis said as the German finished his brief account.

"So you are...ah, just a minute, ah, yes, Jerry Le Godel and Linda De La Haye," Anton said, turning towards the children who were standing alongside the two senior Royal Navy officers.

The two youngsters looked up at the German and noticed his smart peaked cap with the emblem of the imperial eagle at the top front, below which was a double band of almost white rope which made the cap look very official. However, below this, they saw a face that was not hard or cruel as they had expected, but gentle and kind.

"Thank you for saving Erich's life," he said, putting out his hand to shake theirs. "My family and I appreciate your actions greatly."

"Well, to be honest," Jerry replied with modesty, "it was more Captain Lewis and his men who saved him than us."

"Then I thank you too from my heart's bottom," Anton said, turning back to the captain and for the first time getting his English words in the wrong order. "Erich and I are like brothers. Could I ask a special favour, please?"

"I can't see why not," the commodore replied, wondering what he was going to be asked. "As long as it is not the unconditional surrender of Britain you are looking for."

"Oh no, not at all," Anton chuckled. "I have put together photos of family and writed him a letter," the German officer explained. "Would you be allowed to give to him from me?"

"It is not exactly King's Regulations, but I am sure that in the circumstances I can arrange that for you."

"I thank you indeed."

Turning to Jerry and Linda, Anton addressed them, "You two are very brave young people to escape from Jersey. You could both have been shot or blown up by some of my soldiers. I commend your bravery. I am happy to report that your uncle is well and will fully recover from being shot in Guernsey. He will, however, have to spend the rest of the war in a prison camp back in Germany. Thankfully, you are both alive and well despite everything, for which we can only thank God."

"What about my parents, sir?" Linda asked, unable to hold herself back.

"Mr and Mrs De la Haye have been released," replied Anton.

"And what about Mr Pierre Le Blanc?" Jerry asked.

"He waits to go to a prisoner of war camp."

"So he won't be shot?"

"No, as long as he behaves himself."

The commodore interrupted, giving the Oberleutnant a careful but challenging look, "You will ensure that they are fully reunited with their parents and that there will be no repercussions as a result of their escape?"

"As I tried to explain to Oberst Schmettow, we should not, at least I will not, make war on innocent people. My parents brought me up to respect others and I believe it is the right thing to do. I joined the army in 1935 in order to help people and not make war." He looked around slightly uneasily, as if to ensure that no one on the small boat was listening, before adding, "This war is wrong, I know it and you know it, but what can one man like me do to stop it? You, sir, sank the ship my cousin was serving on and no doubt killed the majority of the crew. Did you want to do that? I don't think so at all. I don't want war but sadly our high command does."

Captain Lewis, Commodore Harewood, Sergeant Rennoldson, Medical Orderly Brian Oliver, Linda and Jerry all looked on in silence at Anton's confession. "Once you are back, I will ensure that no further action is taken against you or your parents. You have my word. I am happy to say that they will not now be sent to Germany. Unfortunately I could do nothing to help your uncle, although I tried my best. I am sure he will be looked after in a German prison camp."

"Well, sir," Captain Lewis finally broke the silence. "It's refreshing to know that some in the German forces think like you. Thank you for your confession."

"Now, I think we need to go," Anton added quickly, changing the subject. "I also know that you need to remove your ship out of these waters within the next hour to remain within the confines of the ceasefire. I am sure, however, that our guns will grant you safe passage even if you don't clear Alderney by three a.m. Just keep the flag flying!"

CHAPTER 31

Neither Linda nor Jerry had ever thought of how hard it was going to be to say goodbye to the group of men that had become very special to them over the last few months. Cuthbert and Brian had shown them such amazing care and now suddenly they were going to have to leave them, possibly never to meet again.

As Linda looked towards Cuthbert, the big, burly, but often complaining sergeant, she noticed that tears were welling up in his large brown eyes. Brian pulled both Jerry and Linda towards him and gave them both a friendly squeeze. "Go on, you two," he said as brightly as he could. "It's time for another fine soldier to take you into his care. Remember this, though, I shall never forget these past few weeks with you two as long as I live. You showed me something great and good, and you pointed me to the Lord Jesus. Thank you." Brian's face crumpled, and turning away, he wiped a flood of tears from his face with the sleeve of his uniform.

"Be away with you," Cuthbert commanded, dabbing his eyes with a handkerchief, "before we sink this ship with our tears!"

"On behalf of Commodore Harewood, Sergeant Cuthbert Rennoldson, Medical Orderly Brian Oliver, myself and anyone else who has had the pleasure and privilege of knowing you both over these last weeks, I would like to present you with these," Captain Lewis said as he stepped forward carrying two black books. "These are brand new Bibles that we have all dedicated to you. We thought you might like one each since you have been sharing your uncle's old tatty one."

Jerry and Linda took a Bible each and held them as if they were the most precious things they had ever seen.

"Oh, thank you so much," Linda said, thumbing through the fine gold-edged pages.

"It's leather," Jerry observed, putting the Bible to his nose and smelling its cover. "Real leather. They must have cost a fortune! Wow, thank you so much. These are the most special presents we have ever received, aren't they, Linda?"

Linda nodded in agreement, unable to speak as tears filled her eyes too.

"Oberleutnant Scholz," Commodore Harewood said, looking directly at the German who was about to turn and descend the ladder. "Do you mind if I make a request of you?"

"No, that is fine," the officer replied.

"I'd like to sing a song just for Jerry and Linda before they leave. It will just take a few minutes. Will you allow me to do that, please?"

"Yes," the German said, smiling.

A sailor handed the commodore his accordion. He played two practice notes and then started to sing softly and quietly.

> *God be with you till we meet again,*
> *By His counsels guide, uphold you,*
> *With His sheep securely fold you,*
> *God be with you till we meet again.*
>
> > *Till we meet, till we meet,*
> > *Till we meet at Jesus' feet;*
> > *Till we meet, till we meet,*
> > *God be with you till we meet again.*
>
> *God be with you till we meet again,*
> *'Neath His wings securely hide you,*
> *Daily manna still provide you,*
> *God be with you till we meet again.*
>
> *God be with you till we meet again,*
> *When life's perils thick confound you,*

Put His arms unfailing round you,
God be with you till we meet again.

God be with you till we meet again,
Keep love's banner floating o'er you,
Smite death's threat'ning wave before you,
God be with you till we meet again.

By the time he had finished, a number of *Snowdrop*'s crew had gathered round and a couple of the German sailors had also climbed the ladder to hear what was going on.

"That was very good," Anton said as the last notes of the accordion died away.

"It was beautiful," Linda stammered, wiping the tears from her cheeks. "I really hope, sir, that we will meet you one day at Jesus' feet."

"I have been learning that hymn for the last few days just to sing to you tonight. I really mean every word," Commodore Harewood replied. "Goodbye and God bless you both."

"Thank you all so much," Jerry managed to say as he too struggled to control his emotions. "Come on, Linda, otherwise we might be blamed if this ship is late leaving the area and gets sunk."

With one last little wave, the two trotted down the steps behind Anton and onto the smaller German vessel. Above them, they could hear the familiar voice of Captain Lewis shouting orders. "Mission accomplished. Back to your duties. Start engines. Navigator, give me a course for home."

As the small motorboat pulled away from the side of *Snowdrop*, Jerry and Linda could see three distinct forms leaning over the rail of the ship, waving furiously. No one needed to tell them through the darkness that it was Cuthbert, Brian and Commodore Harewood.

"Good luck," they heard Cuthbert call out.

"God bless," the commodore's voice broke through the darkness.

"The Lord bless thee and keep thee," Brian shouted, "and thank you."

As the two ships rapidly parted, they could see the outline of *Snowdrop* moving in a large arc, turning and heading northwest, away from the Channel Islands, towards the relative safety of the open English Channel.

"We will soon have you both safe at home," Anton said as he smiled at Jerry and Linda, "but please don't go trying to leave the Island again. It might not work out so well for you both next time."

"I don't think that we will be doing that again in a hurry," Jerry replied, "although we have learnt some very important lessons since we left Jersey."

The motorboat made good progress as it sped across the cold grey sea. As Jerry and Linda peered out through the darkness, looking for the familiar outline of their island home, their thoughts travelled back over the weeks that had passed since they had left with Jerry's Uncle Fred. So much had happened since then. Uncle Fred had been shot, injured and captured in Guernsey. They had left him in order to ensure the message got to England, that Adolf Hitler was planning to visit Jersey. As they travelled in a small open boat up the English Channel, they had puzzled about verses underlined in Uncle Fred's Bible where the Lord Jesus had said, 'I am the way, the truth, and the life.' They had been shipwrecked on the Isle of Wight and Jerry had spent some days in hospital before they had been taken by Cuthbert and Brian to London to tell all they knew to some very important people from the armed forces. How disappointed they had been to discover that British intelligence agencies had already found out about Hitler's plan and that they also knew it had been called off.

Then, staying in a guesthouse in London, they had worked out just what those strange verses in the Bible were saying, that the Lord Jesus was the only way to heaven. That understanding had changed their lives and their destinies when they trusted Him as their Saviour.

After that, their case has been brought to the attention of the prime minister, Winston Churchill, who had agreed to provide all necessary aid in order to get them home, especially when he had heard that their families were in danger. Since then, life had been one big blur as they had been bullied, sent to Scotland for training, been involved in a submarine operation, helped rescue some German sailors and as a result were now travelling home in the company of a friendly, helpful and caring German officer. Yes, much had happened since setting out from Jersey!

The three of them travelled in silence until the Oberleutnant spoke as the cliffs of the north coast came into sight. "Do you know what that is?" Through the darkness, he pointed out an archway silhouetted by the vague light of the eastern sky.

"Grosnez Castle," Jerry cheered. "Linda, it's Jersey! It's home."

"Look," Linda pointed, as the hills fell away to a long, flat beach that could just be seen. "There's St. Ouen's Bay, and there is the Martello tower."

"Gordon's Tower," Jerry corrected.

"I never knew it had a name," Linda replied.

"Well, that's what dad calls it anyway," Jerry added. "I think it was named after the chap who built it or something. Oh, look!" He pointed as the boat made its way round the southwestern point of the Island.

"Corbière Lighthouse," Linda whispered in awe. "You know, Jerry, I could almost pinch myself. I just cannot believe that I am nearly home."

"I wonder what Mum and Dad will say when we see them," Jerry said.

As the small boat motored into the harbour in St. Helier, Jerry and Linda, through the misty moonlight, could see the outline of four civilians on the quayside. They didn't ask who they were. They didn't need to.

Epilogue

Mr and Mrs Griffiths

Several times, this delightful and friendly couple survived the bombing of the Isle of Wight. They often watched apprehensively as hundreds of German aircraft flew overhead during 1941 and 1942, preparing to drop their lethal cargoes on the coastal towns of Southampton and Portsmouth. In 1946 they recommenced their bed and breakfast business at Beacon House and were delighted when the teenagers returned with their parents the following year. The couple retired in 1957.

Corporal Brian Oliver

After trusting the Lord Jesus as his Saviour and getting saved, Brian was moved around to various locations as the war progressed, eventually being promoted to sergeant. He was on hand to offer medical aid on 6th June 1944 as the allies landed along the Normandy coast on what became known as D-Day. Sadly, the following day, whilst attending to the injured and dying on Gold Beach, he was killed when a German shell exploded nearby. Brian was posthumously awarded the Military Medal for bravery on land in the face of the enemy.

Michael Meddlum

After the war, when he had turned 16, Michael joined the Royal Navy, and through hard work and determination became a navigation officer on County Class Destroyers before finally retiring in 1985 and returning to the Isle of Wight.

Sergeant Cuthbert Rennoldson

Towards the end of 1944, Sergeant Rennoldson requested to join Force 135, an army unit that was set up and charged with the liberation of the Channel Islands. At 2pm on 9th May 1945, Cuthbert Rennoldson, along with his fellow soldiers and his proud commanding officer, walked from the harbour in St. Helier, Jersey towards the Pomme D'Or Hotel. They were cheered on by the ecstatic crowds who welcomed the liberating soldiers. Cuthbert scanned the eager faces of the hundreds that lined his path, looking for two faces he hoped he would still recognise after four years. Who saw who first was never fully established as a simultaneous chorus of "Linda! Jerry!" and "Cuthbert!" rang out above the frenzied roar of the crowd. He had once again found his charges! The happiness of reunion was tinged with the great sadness that Brian could not also be there to make their joy complete. There was however some gladness when Cuthbert explained to Jerry and Linda that as a result of Brian's witness he too had been saved and was rejoicing as a believer in the Lord Jesus.

Oberleutnant Anton Scholz

Anton Scholz's reluctance to engage fully in the war effort was noted by his superior officers and in 1942 he was sent to the Eastern Front to help German forces at the Battle of Stalingrad. Towards the end of January 1943, he was taken prisoner by the Russian forces, and like thousands of his fellow countrymen, died whilst in Russian captivity.

Commodore Harewood

The friendly, singing commodore survived the war, and after leaving the Royal Navy in 1948, he purchased a croft with his wife at Dunvegen on the Isle of Skye along his beloved west coast of Scotland. Here, he farmed happily, still playing the piano accordion, and occasionally the bagpipes which he finally mastered, until he passed away in 1982.

Captain Lewis

The gallant and friendly captain was lost along with the crew of HMS *Utmost*, a British U-class submarine, on 25th November 1942, whilst on patrol in the Mediterranean.

Linda and Jerry

Both teenagers survived the war despite the great hardships that occupation and finally near starvation brought to all the Channel Islands before final liberation. Jerry married in 1952 and eventually took over his parents' farm, adding tomatoes to the already productive Jersey Royal potatoes his father grew. Linda moved to England after marrying a banker and they settled in the quaint Buckinghamshire town of Beaconsfield to allow her husband easy access to his work in London. Jersey was never far from her heart and when a job opportunity came his way to move to Jersey, Linda made sure her husband took the chance with both hands.

Upon returning to Jersey, after their daring escape, Jerry and Linda sought to find a company of Bible-believing Christians. The Germans had forced all churches with links to England to close. There was, however, one place that the occupiers allowed to continue its activities, simply because it was totally independent, so the two teenagers found their way to Belmont Hall on Belmont Road, St. Helier. It was here they were able to watch in wonder as some German soldiers, attending its meetings, politely hung up their helmets and guns on the coat hooks in order to take their places among the local Christians to learn about and worship the Lord.

Uncle Fred

After being shot in Guernsey and being transported to a harsh prisoner of war camp in Germany, the previously fit and feisty Uncle Fred became a shadow of his former self.

Barely surviving the war, he passed away at his home in Georgetown, Jersey, during the winter of 1946, at the age of sixty-nine, to enter the glory of heaven through his faith in the Lord Jesus Christ.

Return To The Island Of Occupation